No Foreign Land

The Biography of a North American Indian

NO FOREIGN LAND

The Biography of a North American
Indian

**Wilfred Pelletier
and Ted Poole**

c. 1

PANTHEON BOOKS
A Division of Random House, New York

Copyright © 1973 by Wilfred Pelletier and Ted Poole

All rights reserved under International and Pan-American Copyright Conventions. Published in the United States by Pantheon Books, a division of Random House, Inc., New York, and simultaneously in Canada by Random House of Canada Limited, Toronto.

Library of Congress Cataloging in Publication Data
Pelletier, Wilfred.
No Foreign Land: The Biography of a North American Indian.
1. Pelletier, Wilfred.   2.   Indians of North America—Canada. I. Poole, Ted: II. Title.
E99.O9P44   970.3 [B]   73–7029
ISBN 0–394–48033–3

Manufactured in the United States of America

First Edition

In memory of Rosemary Fisher,
who kept the Indian alive.

CONTENTS

Foreword   ix

1 • One of the People   3
2 • The Parasites   55
3 • One of the Strangers   72
4 • Home Is Here   117
5 • The Indian Business   134
6 • The Way Back   156
7 • No Foreign Land   190

Foreword

◻════▷◻════▷◻════▷◻════▷◻════▷◻

THIS BOOK is what is known as a collaboration. But the usual terms "as told to" and "edited by" do not describe how it came into being. The book was grown rather than produced. It proceeded from the ground of a shared humanity, neither by arrangement nor agreement, but through an organic relationship.

The "collaborators" went fishing together, as they have always done whenever they got the chance. Only this time, instead of taking fishing rods, they took a tape recorder along. They stayed for a week in a cabin on the British Columbia coast. They went shopping for food and wine. They split wood and stoked the woodstove. They cooked and ate delicious meals. They washed dishes. In rain and sun they walked in the woods and along the beaches. They threw stones in the sea. And they talked. And the tape recorder ran.

Their talk followed no plan or outline, served no purpose higher than comradeship. For what is more than that? They talked as they had always talked, rambling from reminiscence to speculation to fantasy and nonsense. And their sides were sore with laughing. And as all good talk eliminates the need for speech, there were long stretches of tape that recorded only the crackling of fire and drumming rain on the roof. This too belongs in the book, and it is too bad there is no way to include it.

Later, when each had gone his way—for they live in widely separated parts of Canada—one of them listened to the tapes they had made. He heard the voices of two men: one Indian, the other white, each helping the other to see himself and his own culture more clearly. Each coming by his own path to one sound and one silence.

The rest was just time and work. Selections were made from the tapes, sequences arranged, stories invented, passages written. Gradually a book began to emerge, biographical in form, verbal in style. There were more "fishing trips": a week in an old Ontario farmhouse, ten days in the mountains of British Columbia; more walks, more good meals, more wood split, more talk and more tapes.

There is a reason why we have told you how this book came about. Indians and whites have never been notably successful collaborators. Whites have always swindled Indians and Indians (with good reason) have always mistrusted whites. So it would not be surprising if some people in the Indian community were to say, "Poole is Pelletier's white man," and some people in the white community were to say, "Pelletier is Poole's Indian."

To them we would like to suggest a paradox: Though every man is unique, no man is individual. Individuality is an appearance composed of all the characteristics that seem to separate and alienate one man from another: race, language, color, faith, class, culture, vocation, education, and above all, the "spirit" of competition. But the reality is One. One man. One earth. One life.

Wherever there is fear, the appearance dominates and overshadows the reality. Paranoia accentuates differences and produces "individuals" who live in a polarized world of rights and wrongs, friends and enemies, blacks and whites. And they align themselves in a multitude of opposed configurations and fight over their varying points of view, their "half" way of seeing things.

Wherever two people meet who have experienced and know the reality of oneness, the appearance is transcended and there are no individuals. There is only one. Wherever three such people meet, there is also only one.

This is happening in the world. In the face of incalculable odds, it is the how and the why of human survival.

> Wilfred Pelletier (Baibomsay)
> Ted Poole
>
> *Wikwemikong*
> *July 1972*

Acknowledgments

*To my wife Doris, Ted's wife
Marje Poole, Mrs. Yvonne McRae,
Eugene Peltier, Jack Jones, and
Farrell Toombs; to Gretchen Poole,
for all her typing.
And a special thanks to the people
of Wikwemikong Reservation.*

No Foreign Land

The Biography of a North American Indian

1·One
of the People

□═══□═══□═══□═══□═══□

SINCE I GREW UP and left the reserve I've gradually become
aware of many things about Indian communities, my own
in particular, and about the people who live there. One
thing I now realize is that I was born in one of the most
beautiful places on earth. Manitoulin is the largest freshwater island in the world. It lies at the northern end of
Lake Huron in the path of the eastward-flowing waters
from Lake Superior and Lake Michigan. My village, Wikwemikong, is at the eastern end of the island. It happens
to be the only unceded Indian reserve in Canada because
my people were there before the treaties were made. Most
of the other people on the island were moved there after
the treaties. But even we were not originally from
Manitoulin; we came from the Ottawa valley. We were
Odawas. The whole island was originally set aside by
treaty for the native people of that general area, Ojibway
and Potawatami. But the whites got most of it, eventually,
one way or another.

Manitoulin is a limestone slab, very flat, and the top-
soil is thin in most places. But it grows good hay and
really good turkeys. The coastline of the island is nothing

but coves and bays and white sand beaches. I guess my people settled there not only because of the natural beauty of the place but also because of the easy life. You see, the place was full of deer, and there were all kinds of fish in the lake. And of course, there were all the different birds and animals. Berries of all kinds too, except blueberries—we had to go to the mainland for them. And maple bush. Every spring all the people made lots of maple sugar and syrup.

When I was very young—maybe three or four—my family lived at Wikwemikongsing, or South Bay, as they now call it. I don't remember that house very well, except the upstairs, which was just one big room. There was a window at one end, and that's where my bed was, right by that window. It was winter and I could look out over the top of the frost-forest that grew on the lower half of the glass and see the snow, yellow in the lamplight from the window below, and beyond the light, leafless trees and among them, evergreens bent with the burden of winter.

Even now I have very strong feelings about that whole world outside the window, but I don't know how to describe them. Fear, maybe, or loneliness—I don't know. Maybe my first feelings of that kind. Anyhow, it made me really relish my warm bed—really glad I was inside, perhaps, and not out there.

You see, I would hear the wolves howling and I would lie there all snug and warm and listen to them, and that sound would make me shiver and snuggle down in my bed. Sometimes the howls would come closer. One night I saw deer running through our yard and breaking through the brush down the hill. Not long after, the grey shapes of wolves followed, but they made no noise. And sometimes the lights would come, the northern lights.

Usually they would start down low near the horizon. The trees would stand out sharp and black against the glow. Then a finger would streak up toward the stars, then another, and soon the whole sky would be hung with curtains of moving light. Sometimes they would be colored red and blue and green. And sometimes the lights would come in waves, like a huge silk cloth blowing in the wind.

That was outside the window. I still have strong feelings about the inside of that window, too, and those feelings are not so hard to describe. They are delicious feelings of warmth and security, and they are associated with the sounds of people. My people—my father and mother, brothers and sisters, and sometimes, nearby neighbors moving about in the house below; the sound of the big stove, of someone opening its potbellied door and throwing in more wood; the sound of my father playing the trombone or the violin. He was very good on the violin, and the piano too, but we didn't have any piano in that house. And the smells! The smell of woodsmoke (that was the smell of warmth), the smell of food, and especially fresh bread when my mother was baking.

My grandfather's house was close by, just over a little hill—built on the side of the hill, in fact. It was a big house. Sometimes I went and lived with my grandparents. My most vivid recollections of early childhood center around those visits. At the bottom of the hill you entered through a little gate in the fence around my grandmother's garden. In those days the animals were fenced out instead of in; it took a lot less fence. The back of the house, like its foundations, was built of native limestone, laid up by my grandfather. The back door opened directly into the kitchen, a huge room dominated by a beautiful wood range all covered with shiny, nickel-plated scroll-work. At the back of the kitchen, through a little door cut right into the side of the hill, was a root cellar. It was always cool in there even on the hottest day in summer, and it was just packed with all kinds of vegetables: potatoes, beets, carrots, parsnips, squash, pumpkins. My grandmother would light a lamp and go in there to pick out all the vegetables for supper. Sometimes she would take a big dishpan and put them in that. Sometimes she would just gather her apron up like, all around the bottom, and put them in that. She loved to feed people and she could really cook.

Opposite the kitchen was the dining room and right in the middle of that whole downstairs level was the furnace, because there was no basement, you see. The furnace was round, like a steel drum, only much larger, and there was stonework built up all around it so only the top half showed. It burned wood, huge logs four or five feet long. When my grandfather stoked it, I would stand way back behind him so I could look in and see that big fire in there. Along one side of the furnace and back from it three or four feet, he had built a stone ledge, like a bench. It was covered with bearskins and handwoven rugs. He used to sit there smoking his pipe while we watched my grandmother preparing good things for us to eat.

A staircase divided the kitchen from the dining room and went up to the second story. When you got up there you were still at ground level, only now you were at the top of the little hill. The stairs opened into a big central hall upon which five rooms opened: the little narrow room where I always slept; two other bedrooms; another room that was called the sewing room because my grandmother sewed there; and the room that was the main feature of my grandfather's house, a very large semicircular room where parties were held. It had windows around two-thirds of its circumference and the view was impressive. There was a piano in that room. My grandfather was a good musician, as were each of his sons. They had parties and dances in that room pretty regularly, especially through the winter, and lots of good times.

The room without any corners! My uncle Lawrence used to say that Grandpa built it that way so no matter what you did in that room, the devil wouldn't be able to corner you. He used to say churches should be built the same way, for the same reason.

In some ways I suppose I was closer to my grandparents than to my own mother and father at that time (I was about four years old), which is not at all uncommon in Indian families. But soon that was all changed too. We moved that year, I can't remember just when, to Wikwemikong and a rundown old house, all falling apart and so full of cracks and holes you could see right out through the walls. We got lots of fresh air for a while. The next year my father built a new house.

Wikwemikong: that was my village. And that is where I still go when I go home. I can still remember my first impression of that place. I must have been very small, because I was riding someone's shoulders—my father's, I guess, or my grandfather's. And we were walking at the top, where the hill goes up from the Bay, along the ridge, with all the houses on the slope below us right down to the Bay, and we could see the winding mud roads and little footpaths joining them and the church and people walking like tiny bugs. And the wind was blowing up to us, a strong warm wind carrying all the sounds of the village, dogs barking, kids hollering, someone chopping wood. I can remember that. It was spring. There were still patches of snow under the trees and ice in the Bay, but the leaves were starting and the grass turning green. And it was beautiful. It was so beautiful.

That's all changed now, and I'm changed too.

In those days there were no modern houses. The houses were all made of logs, squared off with a broadaxe and whitewashed. There were picket fences around some of the houses and these were whitewashed too. Everything was neat and clean. Everybody had a garden and you never saw weeds growing anywhere, except the useful ones that you could eat or use for medicine. Even the roadsides were kept brushed out and the graveyard beside the church was always tended. But all that just happened. People did all those things, I guess, just because they saw they needed doing.

I remember one morning I went with a couple of the older men. That morning I woke to the sound of my mother preparing breakfast. I could smell woodsmoke and feel the heat of the stove rising from the kitchen below. The sun was shining in the window at the end of the room, but it was early yet, for it was June. My brother Earl lay sound asleep beside me in the bed we shared. Across the room my younger sister, Yvonne, huddled motionless under blankets, pretending sleep, but I knew she was awake. My other sister, Rosemary, was gone from that bed. She was old enough to help with breakfast. My brother Eugene's bed was also empty.

I loved to wake like this before my mother called us. It meant I didn't feel pushed. I could lie for a little while looking up at the slanted boards of the ceiling, rediscovering a whole world of weird people and animals in the knots and grain patterns of the wood, so that when my mother called from below I was usually ready to get up. But this morning, the smell of hotcakes reached me before my mother's voice, and my stomach took command. I slid from under the blankets, ran across the room, jumped on Yvonne's bed, and bounced the bedsprings four or five times, real hard. When she began screaming I jumped off again, snatched up my clothes in a bundle, and ran downstairs to get dressed by the stove.

We all tried to get dressed close to the stove every morning, but my mother did her best to discourage this because we got in her way. This morning the stove area was already taken by Rosemary, who was having a sponge bath in the galvanized tub that always left <STELCO> branded on your behind, so I had to get dressed sitting on the sofa at the end of the room. Eating my hotcakes, I could hear Eugene splitting the wood that Earl and I would have to carry in until the big woodbox behind the stove was full. Through the window at the end of the table I could see my father's head and shoulders moving up and down as he pumped water into my mother's washtubs.

When the three of us left for school (both Yvonne and Rosemary were still too young), my mother called me back. "Wilfred," she said, "I know it is warm as summer and it seems like you should be able to go barefoot. But *you* know you must wear shoes in school. Now hurry up and put them on. It won't be long till school is over." So I dug them out from where I had them hidden behind the sofa and imprisoned my unhappy feet. As I left my mother called after me once again: "Goodness, boy, where are your stockings?" But it was too late. I was already on my way, kicking stones as I went—the only thing shoes are good for.

It wasn't far to the school from our house in Wikwemikong; you just went out to the road, then up the road toward the church. The school was directly across the road from the church. The two buildings faced each other and neither of them smiled. Where the path met the road, I could see the school. There were no kids in the school-yard—that meant I was late again. But I didn't hurry. If I had learned nothing else in grade one, it was that you might as well be an hour late as one minute. Late was late. A man was coming down the hill toward me. He had a scythe slung over his shoulder and an old straw hat on his head. It was Abraham Wabegijig. I could tell—I don't know how—perhaps by the way he walked. I just knew. When he came even with me, I walked along with him, trotting to keep up.

Abraham was an old man, older than my father. He was a grandfather. The suns and winds and frosts of many seasons had left their marks on his face. His eyes shone out from under black eyebrows, and when he laughed, disappeared completely inside wrinkled folds of skin. He was a small, quick man, the best jig dancer still in the village, and next to my own grandfather, the best storyteller. But he didn't tell the same kind of stories as my grandfather. My grandfather told legends and sometimes what you might call once-upon-a-time stories. Abraham told lies, great big huge lies that got bigger and bigger as he went on and on. Tall tales, I suppose you would call them. But I didn't know that until I was much older.

Alphonse Trudeau stood on his front porch, looking at the morning. He called to Abraham, "Hey, old man, you look like work."

Abraham stopped and rested the butt of his scythe on the road: "I am going to cut the long green hair of my grandparents."

Alphonse looked toward the graveyard within the low stone wall that surrounded the church. He stood on tiptoe as if trying to see the grass and weeds beyond the wall. "It must be a penance you're doing. That grass ain't hardly long enough for a sheep to get hold of."

Abraham laughed: "It's a fine day, Alphonse." And we went on up the hill.

It was seldom, any more, that anyone was buried in this crowded little graveyard. Our neighbor Seraphine said you would have to move your old friends over in order to get into it. There was a newer and much larger cemetery away on top of the ridge. I'd been there too, picking wild strawberries, and had seen the wilted flowers on top of the mounds of fresh mud. But I had never attended a funeral except when Rosemary buried a dead bird in a matchbox and put a cross made of twigs on its grave. She wanted us all to cry. Yvonne cried a little, and so did Rosemary's friend Jeannette, but I couldn't cry and Rosemary was angry with me. The bird stank and should have been buried sooner. Even so, I knew something of death. I had seen a dead horse—old Billy. And I used to ride on Billy's back with my short legs all spread out and hanging onto Eugene for dear life. As he walked, I had felt the heat of his body through the seat of my pants. His vast breathing seemed to heave me up and down. I had strad-dled a mountain of life. Then Billy lay down in my uncle's field and didn't get up again. And I went, holding on to Eugene's hand, and saw the flies crawling in and out of Billy's mouth and the hayseed stuck to his open eyes. And now there was only bones there in that field, and a few bits of Billy's skin.

Sitting on the stone wall, I took off my shoes and lowered my winter feet to the graveyard grass. It felt so good I thought, This must be holy grass. And maybe it was, growing as it did from holy ground. But holy or not, as Abraham swung his scythe, it went down before the blade and the sweet smell of its juice filled the air. The old man's feet were braced well apart. At the end of each stroke he took a small step forward, left foot first, then right. With near-rigid arms he swung the big blade from his shoulders. But the rhythm was never broken. And the swish of the scythe was the sighing of dying grass.

When he reached the back wall of the churchyard, Abraham turned to look at the work he had done. He had left a wake of light green stubble of uniform width and height. He leaned his scythe against the wall and hung his hat on the end of it. Then, pulling a blue bandanna from his pocket, he wiped his face and neck. Standing there with Abraham in the still shade of the maples, I knew that he would die. I had never realized till then that anyone I knew, anyone now living, would someday die. But of course, Abraham was no different from Billy in that way, nor were any of us. Yes, Abraham would die someday, and be buried away in a box just like all the bygone people under our feet right at that moment. The thought of it made me swallow and squint my eyes. Dying is a strange, sad thing.

"Have you been in church saying your prayers all morning, then?" It was Alphonse. Gripping his scythe in one hand, he made a surprising leap and landed with both feet on top of the wall. It was so unexpected—like seeing a bull trying to behave like a deer—that Abraham and I both burst out laughing. He stood there looking at the single swath Abraham had mowed. "I thought you'd have it all done by now."

Abraham grinned. "I left a little for you. I am not a selfish man."

Alphonse's scythe was brand new. Standing before Abraham he held its varnished curves at arm's length. "Factory-made," he said, "store-bought. Even the blade is painted. I haven't tried it yet but I know it won't cut butter. But it will make lots of blisters." He turned and walked to a headstone thirty feet away. "Do you remember my old scythe? Well, this is the man who owned it, the best mower in the whole island in those days." Resting his hand on the headstone which leaned drunkenly toward him, he read the faded inscription: *"Henry Louis Trudeau. Born 1807. Died 1881.* My grandfather. It was made in South Bay, that scythe. Hand-forged in the blacksmith shop. There wasn't another like it in the whole country. He gave it to my father because he was the best mower in the family. And my father gave it to me."

"And," said Abraham, grinning from ear to ear, "I expect your father gave it to you for the same reason."

Alphonse, whose parents had produced nine children —all girls, save one—ignored this jibe. Sighing, he retraced his steps and sat down with us in the shade. "You know Father Reilly?"

"Yes . . ." said Abraham, "from Espanola?"

"That's the one. Last winter he was over here looking for things to put in his museum at Espanola. He came to see me about the scythe. He said it should be—what-do-you-call-it . . . preserved—that it had historic value or something like that and should not get lost or broken. He offered to put it in safekeeping for me."

"So, you gave it to him."

"What could I do? He asked for it."

"Yes," said Abraham, musingly, "old things and new things. Scythes are for making hay. It won't cut any more grass now."

"No, it won't," said Alphonse sadly. "Museums are a

white thing. I don't understand them. I went to the big one in Toronto once. They had stuffed Indians in there. Imagine! They didn't have any stuffed white men."

"I guess not," said Abraham. "Just big fat white people with glasses on, walking around looking and looking and saying, 'Hmmm, so this is what Indians are like,' " and the way he said it was so funny that we all rolled on the grass and laughed till our eyes were full of tears.

Recess came and went. I could hear the kids shouting in the schoolyard across the road, but I stayed out of sight, sitting on the grass with my back against the wall. The truth is, I preferred the company of men. Just to watch them mowing was pleasure enough for me, except that I wished I were big enough to try my hand at it. Alphonse was everything that Abraham was not. Abraham was small and wiry, Alphonse, tall and fat. Alphonse's strength was muscular, Abraham's was rhythmic. Still, one mowed as fast as the other, and as neat, though Alphonse stopped grumbling about his new scythe only long enough to take a new pinch of snoose.

When Dominic Lewis came along, it was almost noon. He leaned on the wall and grinned down at me where I sat below him. "Andrew King got a good catch of fish this morning."

"Yeah?" said Alphonse, not looking up from his work. "Where at?"

"Off Cape Smith. Just inside the rocks there. You know."

"Big ones?"

"No, not so big. But lots of them."

Abraham had left off mowing. He came toward us, mopping his face. Then he took out his whetstone and began sharpening his scythe, working first with quick, short strokes on the tip of the blade. Alphonse joined him and began whetting his scythe. "This thing is like a club," he complained.

Dominic sat on the wall and swung his legs around to our side. "You guys sure look hot," he said. The scraping of the whetstones went on. "What you need is a nice cold beer."

"That would be nice," said Abraham. "Have you got some?"

"No . . . but I've got four dollars. If we had a way to get to Manitowaning, we could get some at the bootlegger's."

Alphonse had a car, an old Chev sedan. But he just went on with his work, saying nothing.

Dominic took out his tobacco and expertly rolled a cigarette. "I was just at Alex Corbierre's before I happened to come up here. They were all drinking beer. It sure looked good. The bottles were all sweating on the outside and running down. Ice cold."

"I have a car," said Alphonse, almost angrily, "but it is out of gas."

Abraham squinted his eyes and tested the edge of his scythe with his thumb. "I think there is a five-gallon can of gas in my boat," he said quietly. Then he gave the scythe one last loving touch-up with the stone.

"Here," said Dominic, hopping down from the wall and taking Abraham's scythe, "let me have a spell." Alphonse also went back to work, but there was little more to be done.

When I was alone with Abraham, I asked him, "What makes the sparks?"

"The sparks?"

"Yes, when you sharpen your scythe with the stone."

"Oh, *those* sparks. Well," said Abraham, settling himself on the wall, "that is a long story." He was silent for so long that I was surprised when he said, "Did you know there was a time when there were no sparks?"

"Not even from fires?"

"No . . . not even from fires. Because there were no fires in those days either."

"How did people keep warm?"

"The sun kept them warm and looked after them just like a mother hen looks after her chicks. People were the children of the sun. In fact, that's what they called themselves: Children of the Sun."

The mowing was almost finished. Alphonse came and sat with us while Dominic busied himself trimming up around the headstones and in the corners of the wall.

Clearing his throat, Abraham continued: "Yes, that was a very long time ago. And the people were very different then. For one thing, they were much taller. Oh, a lot taller. A man would be . . . maybe fifty feet high, or maybe even sixty! Imagine! As high as the trees! And they had three eyes; one in the back of their head for seeing behind them. They had toes on both ends of their feet, so they could run backwards as easily and as fast as ahead. They also had ten fingers on each hand. And of course, they were very strong. Even a woman could pull up a tree and break it over her knee like nothing. And another thing: they could run very fast. They didn't hunt deer like we do. Oh no! They ran them down and caught them with their bare hands."

Alphonse snorted and took another pinch of snoose. But Abraham only glanced at him and went on with his story.

"These people were very happy. They had only one

problem: clouds. They loved the sun because as long as the sun shone they were warm. If the sun shone all day, they could soak up enough warmth to last them through the night without getting chilled. But if the clouds gathered and there was no sunshine for them to soak up, then they would huddle up close together and shiver all night and be really miserable. Well, that's what finally got them into trouble. Because, of course, sometimes it did get cloudy, and if the clouds got thick enough it would rain. Then the people would get all wet and be even colder. When it rained they would shiver so hard you could hear their teeth chattering for a hundred miles. So, you know what they took to doing? Well . . . when they got up in the morning and found it was cloudy, or if it began to cloud up during the day, they'd all gather around in a circle, then they'd reach up into the sky and make a hole in the clouds and start pushing; pushing the clouds back and back, making the hole bigger and bigger until they had a great big hole—maybe as big as this whole island. And that was usually big enough to last them all day."

Dominic, who had now finished mowing, came and sat with us. He took out his tobacco and rolled another cigarette.

"Well . . . you see," said Abraham, "these people got to be pretty good at that. They even had cloud watchers posted around on all the highest hills to give the alarm if they saw a lot of clouds coming. So the people were never caught napping. They could always get out there in time and push the clouds back before they even got close. But with single clouds that weren't too big, those guys never even gave the alarm. They just busted them. Just stared right into the middle of them and pretty soon—*pouf!* that cloud would be gone, shot all to hell. So the sun always shone on the Children of the Sun even though it might be raining all around them. And that's what made the desert. Do you know what a desert is?"

I had only the vaguest idea of what a desert might be, but I nodded affirmatively, not wishing to interrupt the story.

"Anyway . . . out of all this, these people developed a sort of game. It was called cloud chasing. You remember I told you they could run very fast. Backwards as well as forwards. Well, on a nice day like today"—and here Abraham looked up into the sky and we all followed his gaze—"when there were just the right number of nice little clouds around, the men and boys would say, 'Let's have some fun!' Then each one would pick a cloud and at a given signal, they'd start running to see who could catch his cloud first. When they caught a cloud they'd squeeze it, just like a sponge, and all the water would run out. And that's what made all the little lakes. Then they'd bring home those squeezed-out clouds and use them for sponges on Saturday night when they had a bath. And that's where the first sponges came from."

Alphonse settled himself more comfortably on the wall and went on:

Now the Sky was watching all these goings-on and she was getting pretty angry, because she's the mother of the clouds and she didn't like what was happening to her babies. So she called her brother, the Wind. And when he came she said, "Look here, brother Wind, what's going on? Do you realize what these People are doing to my clouds—especially the babies? Have you seen how they're busting them and chasing them and squeezing the life out of them?"

The Wind hung his head and shuffled his feet. "Yes, sister," he said, "I have noticed."

"Well," said the Sky, angrily, "you're the shepherd in charge of my clouds, why are you allowing this to happen? What are you doing all day? Sleeping?"

Now, the Wind was very proud. He did not like being insulted. He drew himself up to his full height and snorted through his nose. All the trees for eight hundred miles were blown down. "Sister Sky," he said, "I'm doing all I can. But to tell the truth, your children are very disobedient. They're always running off in every direction. You know that yourself. When the People start chasing clouds I do my very best to herd every one of them out of harm's way. But even with the help of the breezes, it is just too big a job. Those people are very fast runners and I can't be everywhere at once."

"Well," sighed the Sky, "we have to do something. What do you suggest?"

"I don't know," said the Wind, "except for you to make your children behave better."

"Don't be silly," said the Sky. "They behave like clouds, and that is the best way for them to behave."

"I could go and talk to Old Man Mountain," said the Wind. "He's the wisest person I know. He might know what to do."

When the Wind got to Old Man Mountain's place, he found the Old Man fast asleep. He had to blow in his ear to wake him up. "What . . . ! Who . . . ?" said the Old Man, with a start that shook up half the countryside. "What's happening? Why are you bothering me in the middle of the night?"

"It's not nighttime," said the Wind. "It's high noon."

"Well," grumbled the Old Man, "how's a body to know what time it is when he can't see nothing? Blow these pesky clouds out of my eyes, will you . . . ah . . . that's better. This is the first time I've been able to see anything for months. I had almost forgotten what the world looks like. Now, what's your problem?"

And so the Wind told Old Man Mountain about the People molesting the clouds and about the concern of his sister, the Sky.

The Old Man sat for a long time, looking out over the world, while the Wind kept the clouds out of his eyes. Finally he said, "I am not sure you have come to the right person for advice. You see, I don't hold with clouds because they never give me any peace. They're always sitting on my head, crawling in my ears, and getting in my eyes." The Old Man blinked his eyes slowly. "But there is a simple solution," he continued. "Tell your sister to lift her pesky clouds up higher. A lot higher—beyond the reach of the People. That should make life a lot pleasanter for me too."

The Wind was overcome with admiration. "I wonder why I didn't think of that?" he exclaimed.

"That's what they all say," said the Old Man. "Simplicity is genius."

So the Sky lifted the clouds high above the reach of the People. And the People were very upset, because now it was sometimes cloudy all day and sometimes it rained, so that they spent many miserable nights shivering together and waiting for the Sun to rise.

Then the Sky said to the Wind, "I've heard that our brother the Sun is going on a long journey."

"Is that so?" said the Wind. "Where to?"

"Someplace called the South," replied the Sky. "But the important thing is that he'll be so far away he won't be able to keep an eye on his children. Gather all the clouds you can find. I'm going to cover those bad People with clouds and keep them that way. That should teach them a good lesson."

So that's what happened. The Sun went away on his trip. Up rolled the clouds, and day after day, the sun never shone. And it rained most of the time. Then the rain turned to snow. Both the Sky and the Wind were very surprised when this happened. And so were the People. The snow got deeper and deeper. And that was the first winter. Well, you can just imagine how the People suffered. They ran about slapping their hands together, hugging each other and doing everything they could think of to keep warm. And did they shiver! They shivered so hard they shook themselves right down to the size people are today. But nothing they did was enough to prevent a disaster. Most of them froze to death. Finally, those who were left found a cave and crawled into it.

When the Sun came back from his journey he looked for his children, and of course, he couldn't see anything but clouds. He couldn't even see the world. So he called to the Sky, "Hey, sister, ask our brother the Wind to move the clouds over so that I may greet my children." But the Sky only shook her head and turned away. So the Sun stared very hard and burned up twenty-eight square miles of clouds, just like that! Then the Sky called out to the Wind and said, "Hurry, brother Wind, move my clouds out of the way before they are all gobbled up."

When the Sun saw the world all turned white, he shouted to his sister and asked, "What have you been doing?" But the Sky wouldn't answer. Then he began looking for his children. And he couldn't see one. Not one. Because even the few survivors were all hiding in a cave. He looked so hard that he melted all the snow in one day. Next day the People looked out of the cave and saw the grass growing and the flowers blooming. So they knew that at last it was safe to come out. When the Sun saw his children he was very angry. Again he shouted to his sister, "What have you done to my People? There are hardly any left and they've become so thin and small there's hardly anything left of them." But the Sky didn't answer. So the Sun decided to punish her.

Abraham sat looking at the toes of his shoes. They were cheap brown oxfords that hadn't seen polish since the day he first put them on. From where I sat I could see that the soles were almost worn through. Finally, he looked up and asked, "Do you know what he did?"

"No," I said, anxious only for the story to continue. And Dominic, who was propped up on one elbow behind me, also said, "No."

"Well," said Abraham, with growing confidence, "you know how it is with a fire? A campfire . . . after it's been burning a while and there are lots of coals? If you poke it with a stick lots of sparks fly up? And you also know, I expect, that the sun is a fire? That is all it is, just a big fire. The biggest damn fire in the world. And it has been burning a long time, so there are lots of coals.

"Well . . . the Sun began scratching himself. First he scratched his neck a little bit, and some sparks flew off into the sky. Then he scratched under his arms, and a lot more sparks flew off. Then he scratched his belly with both hands. Then he scratched his head. Boy! there were millions of sparks flying all over the place. And those sparks flew up and burned holes in the sky everywhere. Thousands of holes in the sky. You can't see them in the daytime. But if you look up at the sky at night you can see all kinds of them. And that is where the stars came from."

Looking pleased with himself, Abraham got to his feet, picked up his scythe, and climbed over the wall. Dominic, Alphonse, and I followed. Then a further thought occurred to him. Looking down at me, he said, "Naturally, some of those sparks sort of drifted around and settled down on the world. Just a few. And that started fires going here and there. And the People got scared when that happened and ran back and hid in the cave. But at night they would look out of the cave and see those fires burning and that looked real good. So after a while, they came out again and discovered that standing near a fire was just like being in the warm sunshine. And that was pretty nice, especially at night. They also discovered that the fire ate wood and that if you fed it wood you could keep it alive. And that was the beginning of fire in the world. After that the People were never cold again, no matter how cloudy it got or how much it rained or snowed."

The three men started up the road toward Alphonse's house. I ran after them: "But what about the sparks—the ones that come off the scythe?"

"Oh yes," said Abraham, "when I scratch it with the stone? Well, most of the sparks that landed on the world were no longer hot. They were like ash, I suppose, or . . . or . . ."

"Cinders," said Dominic, trying to be helpful.

"Yes," said Abraham, "that's right. Cinders. You see, before the Sun scratched himself and punished the Sky, there were no stones in the world. Nor rocks either, or even grains of sand. All those are cooled-off sparks from the Sun. They are cold fire like . . . like ice is frozen water," he explained rather lamely. "And when you scratch them on something hard, they give off sparks. Bits of fire. It is like coming to life again."

I went into the schoolyard in time to eat one sandwich and an apple before the bell rang for afternoon class. As

I shuffled ahead in the line-up of grade-oners slowly being swallowed by the school, I saw Alphonse drive by in his old Chev sedan. Abraham and Dominic were in the back seat . . .

Well, that's how different jobs used to get done in the community when I was a kid. And now none of that is going to get done unless it's paid for. They won't do a damned thing any more in that community. "You want us to do it, give us money." All that community was beautiful when I was young. But no one was working for anyone, for the state or for the municipality.

Now, you see, they have a road crew. I don't know how many people are hired there—maybe ten. They have the schools, three schools, and a dozen or two dozen teachers' jobs. Around three or four guys, I guess, working as janitors for the schools. And then they have businesses in the community now, the laundromat, the gas pumps, and a few other things like that. There are three or four stores, one of them big enough so they employ clerks. And then they handle their own welfare. They handle their other services themselves. They have garbage collection now. And I think they have some kind of an engineer who looks after the water. Got water running in there now, at least in some of the homes, not all of them.

They got a guy now who looks after running the shows, the movies in that community and other communities different nights and so forth. And there's all the drivers of buses. How many buses? Eight, maybe, in that community. Another eight people involved there. And there's the old folks' home and there's five or six there, maybe more, because there have to be cooks and someone to look after the old people. All those old people used to be living with their own children and grandchildren and

[24]

they were well taken care of. Now they are removed from their grandchildren and the community is losing its richest resource.

And to take the place of the grandparents, you know what they are doing? They're starting a kindergarten or something, a nursery school. And that's supposed to take the place of grandparents. Maybe better than grandparents: someone is trying to convince them of that, and more people are involved there—trained to do that—youngsters trained to take the place of grandparents. Jesus! What's really happening is that the Department of Indian Affairs is getting those little kids away from the home influence —the Indian thing—at the age of four now, instead of six.

And then they have a health officer—I think, I'm not just sure. And then there's a mailman. And there's a post office, so that makes two of them: one who has the mail routes and the other who has the post office. Holy smoke! There's all that now! And that community's all screwed up.

And the graveyard. I was the one that went up there the last time I was at Wiki, got high on grass, and set fire to the weeds in the graveyard. I burned all that rubbish out of the graveyard, though. Oh yes, I set fire to it! Some of the crosses had caught fire from someone burning the place the year before, so I made sure the crosses didn't burn, but most of the names on the crosses are invisible now, you can't see them anyway. I burned all that stuff. It was burning all over. And some guys had come up, and they had already set fire to the weeds at the far end and burned all that up. The other little graveyard beside the church has all gone to hell too.

But I remember Alphonse, Dominic, Abraham—all those guys who used to go there with their scythes.

[25]

They're old now, those guys. Some of them have gone there for good. In their day people didn't have jobs, but things got done. Those people weren't interested in employment—didn't know what it meant. They had farms and teams of horses—a way of life. And you should have seen the fair days. They'd all gather and bring the blankets and quilts they had made and their basket weaving and pies and pickles and pumpkins and squash and corn —all the things they'd be displaying. And all kinds of other work—sweet-grass and porcupine-quill work. People from Sucker Creek and Mindemoya, from Rabbit Island and Two O'clock; some you didn't see once a year. And then, the foods they'd cook! All that stuff they brought.

You know, it's a funny thing about those fairs long ago. Even when I was a kid there was no competition, no judging—no first, second, and third—no winners and no losers; just a display of what you had produced. The big attraction was people—people you hadn't seen for a long time—and getting caught up on all the stories. They don't have the same kind of fair any more. Maybe it's just that people aren't growing things and making that stuff so much now. But I think what really killed it was the church began promoting it, and pretty soon if you set up a booth, they wanted everything you took in. Then they started running Bingo games and stuff like that . . . and so the old fairs are gone.

People are becoming isolated from each other, becoming individuals in a community setting. Although individuality was always there before, it was not an alienating individuality. It was also community, and now that's not happening any more. And the work isn't getting done, the community isn't as clean. It's all going to hell

—everything. You know, a guy gets burned out now, they look to Indian Affairs or somebody else to build the guy a home. When I was young, that guy got burned out and two days later he was living in a house. The community had one up for him. And it was made of hand-hewn logs, whitewashed maybe, but never painted. So it's really . . . really different.

And of course, that means that the kinds of houses people live in now are different. When the government puts up a house for you, they even want it painted every year because it isn't your house, it's government property. And those houses are all partitioned off so the people living in there have a whole different experience of living and being together. Space and how you use it is pretty important. In all those old houses, I can remember, you had complete privacy, even in one room. We all slept in one room upstairs in our place. Downstairs we had a living room and a kitchen. But we had complete privacy there. The way that happened is, you isolated yourself in a room full of people. People just knew you were there, and if you were going to do something—well, say, if you wanted to sponge-bathe, you just undressed by the basin of water and you sponge-bathed right there. All the kids, and the adults too. And nobody paid any attention to you. It was just a part of what happened.

You see, we weren't aware of something called sex. I mean, to be curious about it; to think, Well, that's an immoral thing or that's a moral thing, or to look at it any way. Like when growing up there was a time we were interested in girls, but we didn't go looking for a girl. It just happened, sort of. When there was a dance all the girls would go by themselves and the boys the same, and you just ended up with a girl after the dance was over.

Our language didn't have bad moral connotations about sex, so it was freely talked about by all ages.

I guess maybe my parents used to have sexual relations right in bed next to us and we'd be sleeping with them and there was never any kind of thought about that. But even this is changed in some homes, I guess, and people now see that as a kind of behavior that shouldn't go on. I don't know, but I think that probably has a bearing on families breaking up. Anyway, that's a whole white thing—privacy from your own family. I expect most whites would find it hard to imagine how you can have privacy with your family unless the house is segregated into rooms and everyone has his own room. But I've noticed too that people brought up the Indian way, when they leave their family and the reserve, really isolate themselves. Most girls I knew, when they left the reserve, wanted a private room all to themselves. I don't understand why they do that, because after a while they usually do end up living with someone else. It may be that it is just the novelty of having a room all to themselves that's attractive—I don't know.

And another thing about houses: take Isaac's parents, for example, a beautiful new, modern house was built for those two old people. The whole idea seemed to be to make life easier for them. But what does the old man say to me? It's a whole different way of life. What he says is, "Now I'm useless. My wife just pushes the button and the lights go on." He says, "I can't fill the lamp no more." And he says, "She just turns another button and the house gets warm and I can't—I'm no good any more. I can't go and cut wood and so I can't be part of the house. She turns another button and cooks all the food and everything; turns the tap and the water's there—I can't go and get no water. I'm just no good any more."

He's useless. See, his whole role has become just a putdown thing. Life has not been made easier for those old people, it has been made meaningless. That old man's experience of going to the well, of chopping and piling wood, filling the lamps, all those things that keep a house going have been taken away from him. I suppose he might get a set of blocks to play with and try to learn something, I don't know—keep himself occupied or busy. Well, what are you going to do with a guy like that? He's got to have something. The whole emphasis of progress is on everything except the human being. It's like progress is out there somewhere, so there's no progress in terms of self. But all there is, is self. And what has been taken from that old man is little pieces of himself. If you take away enough of those, there is no self left. Just a shell. I suppose the dominant society would call that old man's chores work. And they think work is bad, something to get out of.

I remember when a wagon would be passing through town and a lot of us kids—fifteen or twenty of us, maybe, would all get on that wagon and go to weed a guy's potato garden or put up hay, and it was really great. I guess it was because we didn't look at that work as something we *had* to do. Not only that, we had a lot of fun while we were doing it. And you just knew there was going to be some food at the end of it; you'd always get a good meal, you knew that. It didn't matter if a guy went out twenty-five miles away or something, you'd just sit there bouncing along and the first thing you knew you'd find yourself way the hell out, out past Buzwah or Kaboni and even as far as South Bay. It didn't matter if you didn't come back. You'd sleep out there—there'd be some place to sleep. But you'd participate in whatever was going on. Maybe the guy was just going out to get lumber or something, to a sawmill out there; we'd pile on a big pile of lumber and then we'd sit on the lumber pile coming back the next day. And nobody asked you, either—they never said, "Where were you yesterday?" or anything like that.

One thing I liked was that those rides were excursions through the community, visits with all kinds of friends. We'd stop and talk to the Manitowabis, Wabegijigs, Shawandas, Trudeaus, and many more people along the way. I remember playing with different kids, exchanging stories, wrestling, being shown all the local things of interest, maybe riding horses while the men talked. Old Sam Jocko's place was a sort of halfway point and everyone seemed to stop there, maybe because he always fed everyone who came around.

Sam was a good storyteller, so after they had eaten, everyone would usually gather around to hear a good story. The characters in old Sam's stories were always people we all knew or had heard of—our own grandparents or uncles or aunts—and often we kids would learn things about them that we'd never heard before. I remember one story he told about old Jackson and my grandfather, Joe Peltier.

Old Jackson was cutting wood with a couple of young guys out back of Two O'clock somewhere. Times were hard then and a lot of people were cutting wood. Most of them worked for Irwin, who owned a store in Manitowaning, and part of the deal was that they could get rations at his store. Irwin had hired my grandfather to sort of oversee the whole operation as he knew all the people in Wikwemikong. This time my grandfather just happened to be away when old Jackson showed up in Manitowaning for his rations, so Jackson went in to see Irwin himself.

"I want rations for four," he said.

"What are their names?" Irwin said. "I have to write them down in the book."

"Well," old Jackson said, "there's Eli, Frank, myself, and Bekajibe."

"Oh yes, that's four," Irwin said. "And how do you spell that last name?"

"I don't read or write," Jackson said. So he got his rations for four and left town. When Joe Peltier got back, he was told that Jackson had been in and got his four rations.

"Well, he has only two boys," Joe said. "That makes three all together. What names did he give you?"

"There they are, although I don't know how to spell that last name." So next time my grandfather went out Jackson's way, he called in on him. They were eating at the time, and Jackson took two slices of bread out and put lots of butter on the bread and gave it to his dog. He then said, "Well, it's only right that he eats well too. After all, his name is in that very important book in Manitowaning."

So of course, Joe Peltier then knew what Jackson had done. He asked, "What is the dog's name?" and Jackson told him, "Bekajibe."

We really laughed at the story, and Sam said, "That happened to your grandfather." That incident sure made me feel good. Suddenly I felt very close to Sam and grateful to him for telling that story. I guess it was a whole identity thing; he seemed to be acknowledging me and telling me who I was. The important thing was being together with your friends; what you did wasn't so important. Fun always came from being together, all sorts of horseplay, and no matter what we did I don't remember adults interfering very much. Oh, the odd time somebody would go by—well, either they'd laugh at us or they'd join us or else they'd just shake their heads.

We played with dogs and cats and horses and cows—even pigs—because those animals were always around. Most of our play just happened, like chasing squirrels, for example. We'd be playing a game, maybe, or working somewhere in a field and we'd hear a squirrel chattering. It might be close by or it might be way off in the woods, it didn't matter, we'd drop everything and take off after that squirrel. When we got to where we thought the squirrel was, lots of times there wouldn't be a sign of it. Not a sound—nothing. Then we'd all stand perfectly still, waiting and searching the treetops with our eyes. We never had to wait long. That squirrel just couldn't stand it. Suddenly he'd let loose and really cuss us out. That's the way it always seemed to me, but maybe he was only playing with us, because as soon as he gave himself away, he'd take off through the trees and us after him on the ground. Maybe somebody would have a slingshot or bow and arrows and they'd try to hit him. Sometimes the squirrel would isolate himself in a tree, and if there were enough of us we'd shake him out. Then we'd all scatter because if that squirrel fell on you, as sometimes happened, he'd bite. He was mad. What I remember most clearly about all that was the laughter, the screaming laughter of excitement. All over a little squirrel. You'd have thought we were chasing a mountain lion.

When I think about it, all the things we got the most fun out of were dangerous. Things you'd probably never do on your own, if you were alone. Like the bees. But that was so dangerous it wasn't just play; it was more of an initiation thing.

I remember the first time it was my turn to worry a

bees' nest—a hornets' nest. There was one of those rail fences that came to a corner and the nest was right there, just over the fence. I had to go in the same yard as the nest. Well, I couldn't go around the one way because there was a house over there blocking it off, and besides, the grass was real high in there, a lot of twigs and things. But on the downhill side it was all open field. There was also a dog on the other side belonging to that house, and I didn't think it was very friendly. So when those bees—those hornets—came for me I'd have to get over the fence before I could run. No other way. And all the others were already on the right side of the fence.

Now this is what those guys had done: they'd worried that nest before I got there, so the bees were all kind of sensitive. And I got over there, over that fence, and I ran by the nest a couple of times. That was okay. Next time I went by I kicked it a little bit, climbed over that fence, and fell on the ground. Then I rolled head over heels and stood up and ran. But nothing happened. Well, I guess I went over four times, and I had to do this. And the last time I flipped it—you know, with a stick. I flipped it in the air.

Well, when I did that the bees came out of there, a whole swarm, and I went over that fence—I don't remember even touching it—and I ran down through the field as if the devil was after me. All the other kids began running and hollering, and of course, the bees were after them. Every now and again you had to take evasive action, and so you would roll and dive through the grass and then get up and run some more. The ones who were a little more experienced in this whole business would stop at times and look around to see if the bees were still following; and some of them were very good at it, some of them never did get stung. The field sloped away down toward the Bay, and some of us ran all the way down there and right into the water.

I said this was a sort of initiation, and that's true. But it was one of our greatest sources of fun. Whenever we found a bees' nest, a whole strategy, a whole thing would develop around that. On the occasion I'm speaking of, I only got one sting. Right on the ass. But sometimes we got stung quite badly. Of course, we were forbidden to play with bees, but whenever we found any nest there was just no way at all we could resist this, and we'd keep going back there and fooling around until we agitated the bees or hornets to the point where they took after us. Later on, when I was older, it was the same with bears. We had even more fun scaring bears. But sometimes they scared us.

I once brought some bees to school, but I didn't mean to. We were supposed to draw or paint something from nature, from environment, so everyone brought in leaves or plants and things like that. I brought in this bees' nest. I remember it was late fall, there was even a little snow on the ground, and when I found this nest there were no bees around it at all. It seemed like an old, deserted one. But I didn't just break it off and carry it away. I fiddled around with it some, and when no bees came out I finally snapped off the branch it was on and brought it in. Well, the teacher hung it up on a nail above the blackboard. After a while the guys started shooting spitballs at it. Then a bee came crawling out the end of the thing and we all saw that. That started a whole barrage of spitballs, and the teacher got mad and told the boys to stop that. But she never once looked up at the nest because her whole attention was on those bad boys. Suddenly those bees came to life and really swarmed out. Stampede! Some of the guys went out through the window. The girls went out the door. One or two girls got stung, but the teacher, who was the last one out, got three stings. And I got hell. Maybe because I didn't get stung at all. One of her eyes was completely closed and she had two great big red lumps on her neck. Did she ever lay into me! And I didn't know there was anything in that bees' nest. I didn't!

My whole life was one of being blamed for things. My brothers Eugene and Earl and all of them used to do all kinds of things, and I always got blamed because I was the bad boy. Of course, I loved that, too—I lived off that. Somebody would do something really bad and it wasn't me at all, and they'd blame me, and I'd sit there feeling real good that I was being blamed. It wasn't me, and I got blamed all the way through. You see, I did most of the "no-no" things in the open, in front of my parents or other people; I was never sneaky about anything I did. Like when I was sent to the store for a can of coal oil, I'd do a little fire breathing on the way home. I'd just take a mouthful of coal oil, light a match, blow that coal oil across the flame, and fire would be shooting out of my mouth, a big long flame. This was forbidden because it was dangerous, but all the kids did it. Most kids would hide someplace and do it, but not me. So I learned how to use all those things to work for me. Eugene and Earl would go in the cornfield or behind the shed to smoke, but not me; I just lit up in front of my parents. Maybe this is why when something happened I got blamed, because they could see how bad I was in the open. Even to this day sometimes I hear different people telling stories about me when I was young. I know it wasn't me who did it, but I take the blame all the time. I have to laugh at them because it wasn't me that time, it was somebody else. But they say, Wilfred did this and Wilfred did that.

That's a funny thing and I still think about it a lot, that

whole blame thing. Maybe it had something to do with identity, unless I was a—what-do-you-call-it, one of those people who enjoy being punished?—a masochist. But I don't think so. I just thought of myself as the "bad boy," I guess, the one who gets blamed.

Kids don't have any identity. Little kids don't even refer to themselves as "I" or "me." They use their given names. They don't have any "I" consciousness. And in a tribal community identity is never a source of anxiety. Kids just grow into people. But in white society I don't think kids are allowed to just grow. They're processed into vocational components, and *that* becomes their identity. And they have to create that—and go on and on creating and maintaining it. That's what schooling is all about. They aren't supposed to be able to live without it. In fact, it's called a livelihood.

But the truth is, they're dying from it. Dying from not knowing who they are, and killing each other. Like, if you see a guy as a category of some kind and he sees you the same way, then you can do all sorts of things to each other that no human would ever do to another human. I don't know who called the city, the "Stranger Society," but he named it right.

◻▭◻▭◻

I was a pretty big boy before I knew I was something called an "Indian." And that was a category put on me by whites. Oh, I had seen lots of whites. There were some who lived right in our community, but I thought of them as priests. There were sometimes others who came to the villages too—I remember there'd be some of us showing those people around when I was just a young fellow. But just knowing they were whites and different didn't make me aware I was Indian.

One of the differences I noticed was that they would talk and talk and *talk*. My father talked some too, but not as much as those guys would, and my mother didn't say anything. It was hard to get used to. But even though I couldn't keep track of it all, I thought it was great. Even in later years when I used to hear those intellectual arguments, I thought that was great. I don't think that now; I think it's a disease.

I remember one guy who used to come around selling apples. We had apples galore, all free. They didn't belong to anybody, they belonged to the community. You could go into any yard and help yourself, and there were trees growing all over the place. People would say, "Go down there, the other side of the barn. That tree with the big red ones, they're really good." Anyhow, this guy would come and sell apples. Well, people would buy them to accommodate the guy. But he had an orchard and he'd have this car loaded full of apples. He used to come and spend some time at our place, and we used to hang around and smell those apples in that car. Just stand around that car, and boy, did it ever smell nice! He was one of the whites that came into the community. The others were salesmen or visitors. But all those people came to my father's place because he was working in a logging business. I'm not sure if he was doing that at the beginning, but he did work in a logging business for quite a while after we moved out of that little town. They'd come and talk, talk, talk, talk. And priests! Never shut their mouths, never. I used to hear priests ask a question and before anyone could answer they would ask another question and answer it themselves most of the time. It was like using us or having us there just so they could talk to themselves. They would just go on and on and on, and after they'd leave the people would say, "I wonder what they came here for? I wonder what they wanted?" Well, those clergy never got anything out of it, I guess. They couldn't have. Different priests would come different times, and when the priest left they'd say, "This one comes and talks two hours. Do you understand him?" "No, I don't know what he's talking about." Then they'd go on talking in Indian and say, "Well, he said something about Bingo or something, I don't know. Oh well, somebody'll come and tell us." And that would be the end of that.

I also remember when others used to come to teach the older women what to do in the community, like cooking, sewing, and housekeeping. I don't know what kind of teachers they were—they'd call them "sister" anyway—and they were never invited, they just came. They were old maids, you know, and they were always wanting to show the Indian women the proper way to do things—like peeling potatoes, for instance. Good God, the potato was invented by the Indian! Indians developed the potato and have been using it for God knows how many generations, not just a couple of hundred years.

Those sisters, or whatever they were, assumed Indians didn't know anything. But I never heard my mother or any of those Indian women offer an argument. They'd just say—after the sister had left—"Now we'll go back to our own way." And they would laugh and say, "Oh, they're throwing the best part away." They always used to say that: whenever they'd see somebody fixing anything fancy, they'd say it was throwing the best part away, fixing the food to look nice but without any nourishment because that was either in the peeling or someplace else.

I realize now that when these people came into our house—those priests and people from the church—they didn't come as visitors, they came as instructors. And they didn't talk like friends, they spoke like textbooks. And I can see now, too, that all white institutions are based on talk. The structure always requires one person to get up in front of a lot of other people and talk . . . and talk . . . and talk. That one person is supposed to be the one who knows, and all the others don't know. It's the same way in church, the same in school. And they always have a desk in front of them, or a pulpit—between them and the people. That's for protection, I guess, in case the mob out front finds out the truth. They're supposed to be the ones who know. But they don't even know enough to shut up and listen. And I don't just mean listen to someone else talk. Indians know how to listen to silences. Whites are panicked by silences.

▣▭▭▭▣▭▭▭▣

You know, school was a crazy experience for me. I doubt if I learned anything kids are supposed to learn there. I learned to read and write, but I wonder now if I really did learn those things in school. For one thing, I was never there that much. I think I did learn a lot about how to cope with institutional structures, how to screw up authority and stuff like that. Of course, I realize now that the reserve school was not really a school at all, it was a correctional institution. Indians had to be turned into nice, obedient, English-speaking copies of white children before they could be taught anything. And for those poor teachers, I guess that was an impossible task.

I realize too that I was really very lucky. At that time hundreds of little Indian six-year-olds were rounded up every year and sent off to some distant Indian residential school. For the next ten years of their lives those children were condemned to spend ten months of every year in an institution, totally removed from their parents and grandparents, totally cut off from the community. Well, that didn't happen to me so I can't really talk about it, but from everything I've heard, I know I was really lucky.

There is no question that school is a very different experience for Indians than for whites. For whites, the school is really an extension of their own culture. But for Indians, the school is culturally foreign, just as the language used in the classroom is a foreign language. In an Indian community people who speak out, for example, or who are aggressively competitive are regarded with silent disapproval. That's why I doubt that there'll ever be any great numbers of successful Indian students.

For whites, school is the accepted passage from childhood to adult status. For Indians, it's a big detour that takes you out of reality, out of life. Even in grade one I think we all knew we were going to cut wood and fish and trap and hunt and farm all our lives, and we'd already learned a whole lot about those things by *doing* them, working right along with our folks. So I guess in one way we were a lot more grown up than white kids that age. But from a white point of view, maybe we were a lot less mature, less reliable. We played hooky a lot, especially in the spring, and we never seemed to be able to get to school on time even though we were punished for lateness.

For me, the school was a trap. Once they got you in there you weren't supposed to get out till they let you out. And the teacher was a trapper. You spent the whole day trying to keep from getting trapped. And sometimes things happened—I don't know—just seemed to get tighter and tighter till something snapped. Then there'd be a bunch of guys going out through the window. That window was our first line of retreat, and when that happened it just seemed you couldn't help it even though you knew you'd catch hell the next day when you came back. Looking back on it, I think those sudden flights from the classroom were usually triggered by so much pressure being put on one person that he'd sort of break. For some kids, just becoming the center of attention was more than they could bear. When the teacher would ask Jerry Wabegijig, for example, to stand up and answer a question, the whole class would suddenly become very still. You could just feel the tension radiating off that guy and filling the room because Jerry was kind of crazy. I don't mean really crazy—he had all his marbles—but he was wild. He had a wild look in his eye, and you never knew what he'd do. And she'd say, "Now, Jerry, I would like you to answer this question. You don't *have* to answer it, but if you know the answer . . ." and she'd come on really nice like that. Jerry would look at her with those wild eyes and he'd look at the window. And sometimes he'd take a notion to answer. If he did, that would be really strange, because usually he'd just stand there getting tighter and tighter until he exploded. And most of us were so totally involved in his feelings that we'd explode too.

Now I think that school, like all schools, was like a dam built across the natural flow of childhood. That river of youthful energy was forcibly channeled into the school, and what you *had* to learn, more than any other thing, was submission—to allow the energy that belonged only to you to be controlled and directed by someone else. When you stepped into the school you were confronted by a boss adult. You were also confronted with masses of departmentalized information *about* the world, about nature. You were trapped between the teacher and a wall of abstractions. Beyond that wall lay the real world, the material world, always waiting, beckoning to you, and there wasn't supposed to be any way of getting back to it except by working. You were supposed to attack the wall, subdue the information; master it by taking it all apart and putting it together again.

This may be an exaggerated generalization, but from where I stand now it seems to me that the object of that whole system is to bring about a displacement. I don't know if white kids ever experience school as a world apart, but that's the way it seemed to me. I realize now that I was supposed to feel challenged; I only felt threatened. When the teacher talked about history, it was all from a book and all about strange places and strange people. Nothing to do with us. She never talked about her personal history, the only thing she really knew. When she talked about science or reading or math, it all came from someplace else or somebody else. She was a real live person and I would have liked to get to know her, but that couldn't happen because she saw herself as only an information center. A distorted one, at that, because she was forcing what somebody did to her onto me. The contrast between that classroom and the world outside was so great that when you stepped outside it took your breath away. Out there, for one thing, there were no boss adults, unless you just happened to run into a priest somewhere. I didn't stand in opposition to my parents, I stood with them. And the people of that community were aligned *with* the world they lived in, not against it. When the men went out to cut wood they didn't confront the trees; they weren't into subduing the forest. They were just a bunch of simple people putting up some cordwood. No big deal.

Now I've lived long enough to know that what those

[42]

who go all the way through the school trip and graduate with a degree are supposed to achieve is objectivity. They pride themselves on their objectivity. Which means that, to them, all things are primarily objects. They themselves are objects. What differentiates them from other, less educated people is their ability to eliminate feeling from experience. Thousands of people have been conditioned in that way and I suppose it has been productive of unbelievable technological successes, but not without a price. As is now generally realized, it has also been productive of environmental disaster.

The only thing I can remember that I really liked about school was when the teacher would read us a story. There was nothing I liked about the rest of it. The things they taught seemed to me just a bunch of bullshit that didn't mean anything. It wasn't anything. They'd have social studies. They'd talk about plants and flowers, and sometimes they'd all go on a big hike to gather specimens. Me, I'd already left school. I'd be out there up to my ass in the flowers they were studying about. I'd be riding a horse and I'd meet them out there. And she'd say, "Well, are you coming back to school? You've got to get back there." And her other eye would be on the horse, and I'd say, "Yes, teacher, I'm coming back. I'll be right back," and we'd ride off, my friend Leland and I.

One time the teacher called us in and gave us the strap, Leland and me. Leland wasn't even going to school that year, but he got the strap too. And he took it and laughed, and that made me laugh. Then she started to cry, and I felt so sorry for her because she used to do nice things for me. She really used to help me with my schoolwork and she didn't ask me too many questions, or asked me only the easy ones. The truth is, I liked most of those teachers even though they tried to suppress me. I guess I understood they had to do that: it was their job. Like forbidding us to speak our own language and punishing us if we did, even if they caught us talking Indian outside the school altogether. That was done to all us kids. But that was only at the reserve school, the one run by the church. When we moved off the reserve and went to Ten Mile Point, the school there was different. That was a public school. They suppressed us in different ways.

We left Wikwemikong in the spring when I was ten or eleven and moved to Ten Mile Point, where my father owned a tourist lodge. That fall we went to a little one-room school. We registered there, the five of us, Rosemary, Yvonne, Eugene, Earl, and me. The school was almost three miles away and we had to walk that every day, going there and coming back. That long walk was quite pleasant in spring and fall, but in winter the wind blew off the lake, across that long, flat stretch of road, and sometimes the snowdrifts were so high we walked level with the telephone wires. We had both snowshoes and skis and used whichever was best, depending on conditions.

It was at Ten Mile Point school that I first experienced discrimination. We were Catholics, my brothers and sisters and I, and we were also the only Indians. That area was totally Protestant, and I guess there was a lot of religious feeling around. We were the only Catholics in the school. We got into some big religious arguments with the other kids at noon hour and recess, especially Rosemary.

Throughout the winter at that school we were supposed to have a hot meal and the kids helped the teacher prepare it. Well, they wouldn't let us help with that; we couldn't make tapioca pudding or fix the soup or any-

[44]

thing. They wouldn't even let us wash dishes. Now that wasn't because we were Catholic; that was because we were Indian. We weren't allowed to go near the food because we were dirty Indians and we'd contaminate it or something. We were pushed right out of the school, and had to eat our lunch in the woodshed.

Boy, we suffered that first year; we didn't fight back much, we just took everything. But the next year we came back and I'm telling you, that was the end of that. We fought with those guys, and we beat every one of them too. When they'd play ball, we'd be excluded. There were just five of us, but I wouldn't stand for that—none of us would. I found I could beat the tar out of the kids my size and even some of the bigger ones. I was a tough little bastard anyway. So was Rosemary; she could lick all those girls there and half the boys. So we just took the place over. They used to play a game there—Anti-I-Over, or something—where they'd throw the ball over the school-house to the other side. As soon as we tried to get into that game and play with them, they'd quit. It was the same with every other game: every time they started something we'd move in and take over. Then they'd quit. Finally they decided to play with us, only one or two at first, then more. But some of them never did accept us, really.

But inside the school was a different thing—that never did change. In there the teacher was in charge, and we were all put together at the very back of the classroom. When they had a school play, we weren't involved. We were left out of it. I had one small part in one play, that's all. And Rosemary had one part too, but the rest didn't. Though we had a problem with the kids, it was the teacher who always suppressed us. As far as the kids were concerned, once we took a stand and fought, some of them came over to our side. But I finally solved the schoolroom problem too. That third year I just played hooky every day. I didn't stay there at all. Anytime that the teacher said, "No," I'd say, "I'm going anyway," and I'd just pick up my stuff and I'd leave.

But she liked me, that teacher, even though I played hooky. She sent me home one time. She said, "Don't you come back here until you learn to behave." So I went home and I wouldn't go back to school. A week later she came and talked to my mother. "Well," my mother said, "Wilfred's here. I don't know why he's not going to school. He says he's not supposed to go to school, he was thrown out of school." The teacher says, "Oh no, I just told him that he was not to come back until he learned to behave." And so my mother called me. I had been listening to all this. I came out and she said, "That's not what you told me. The teacher said that you're not to come back until you learn to behave. You told me that you weren't to go back to school." So I said, "Yes, Mom, the only thing is, I haven't learned to behave yet." I stayed out three weeks that time and I kept telling my mother, "I haven't learned to behave yet." Well, that was pretty smart-alecky. My mother was so mad at me that she made me do all kinds of washing and other chores while I was home. She really kept me busy. I had to split wood and I worked like a son of a bitch. I was glad to get back to school, finally, so I could play hooky.

Today there is a lot of concern about sex education. And that makes me laugh because any honest person knows that you can't learn anything about sex from books

or classes. You can only learn about it by doing it. We had
sex education at Ten Mile Point. It wasn't on the cur-
riculum, but we had it.

Directly across the road from the school there was a
farm, Perkins' farm. There were three Perkins kids in the
school. Mr. Perkins had a bull, and all the farmers in the
country around about brought their cows to Mr. Perkins'
bull to be serviced. Whenever anything interesting began
to happen across the road, the whole class became restless.
There was only one window on that side of the school, so
most of the kids would begin craning their necks trying
to see better. Eventually, some would stand up and then
begin edging up or down the aisle toward the best places
to see from. Some of the bolder ones would end up going
right to the window and looking out. Meantime, most of
the girls pretended that nothing was going on. But after
a while they would be glancing sideways at each other and
giggling. The teacher also tried to ignore the whole thing.
She went right on with the lesson, her voice getting
louder and louder and her face redder and redder. Finally,
she would have to order the boys back to their seats. Then
she would go and stand in front of the window and continue the lesson from there. There was a blind on that
window, but the window was very tall and the blind
didn't fit—it only came down halfway. Usually the
teacher would pull the blind down too. I don't know why
she did that. Maybe it made her feel better to think she
was doing everything she could to keep us innocent children from seeing all that dirty stuff across the road.

When recess time came, it was always plain that the
teacher really didn't want to let us out into the schoolyard.
She even succeeded a couple of times in keeping us in
right through recess. But I guess our resentment against

her for doing this was so great that it wasn't worth it. So at recess or noon hour, out we would go to see the big sex show. The girls skipped rope or bounced balls as usual, but they stayed on the side of the school nearest the road. Most of us boys lay in the grass opposite Perkin's barnyard and watched the show. When the bell rang for us to return to class, hardly any of us boys would go back into the school. Usually, the teacher would come out after a while and scold us and try to herd us back to classes. But sometimes she didn't bother.

Well, that was sex education at Ten Mile Point school. Or part of it. The ridiculous thing is that we were all farm kids. We were used to seeing animals involved in the sex act, all kinds of animals. We saw it all the time, but that didn't seem to make it any less exciting. Why was all that so fascinating?

Sex education for adolescents, that is, for children who are old enough to know and therefore *must* be told something, illustrates most of all that in white society there are areas of human experience that are off limits, mystery areas that are not nice and, among decent people, are never openly discussed. I know all that prudish dishonesty is breaking down, but the parents of most children now in school are still hung up on sex. Their concern is not that their children learn all about sex, but rather, that they learn sex is essentially bad and must never be indulged in except with the official approval of the church and the state. Of course, all official instruction on the subject implies very strongly that sex is solely for purposes of reproduction. The fact that there are areas of experience that children are forbidden to know about, where learning is blocked and experience discouraged, makes a mockery of education.

The so-called generation gap is created and maintained mainly by adult liars who are so dumb they don't know you can't con kids. When adult lying becomes official, even scientific as in many school texts, the entire concept of public education is discredited, the snow-job melts in a springtime sun of truth, and the kids drop out in order to begin learning something which has some relevance to life and living.

There are many lies which are just sort of built into society and which all kids are encouraged to accept and believe. Sex is one of these. Sex is bad—dirty. Sex should be avoided. Sex is forbidden. All that is a big lie. I found sex was good, good to watch and good to experience. It never seemed dirty to me, only beautiful and natural. The further I moved out into white society, the less I could understand why whites were so afraid of sex. But what I saw was consistent because they were against life and against nature, always. So how could they be in favor of natural behavior?

All the memories of my school days are colored with sex, and I know I was no different in that respect from the other kids, boys and girls both—that was normal. Sex was the dominant theme in my life, overriding everything else. Every hour of every day I burned with it. It was a tide of energy too great, too magnificent for me to manage. But I tried to ride it just the same.

Energy and the classroom. The confining desks, the rigid regulations, the sterile subject matter. I wonder if that teacher ever had any idea what she was trying to control? I wonder, when she was so busy trying to force all that dead information into us, if she ever realized what we were really burning to know all about? If I had to give that whole sex feeling a name at that time in my life, I'd call it curiosity. But within those four walls there was not a word, not a whisper about sex. You'd have thought we were all as smooth between the legs as store dummies.

But in spite of the prohibition against sex and life within that school, life and sex were constantly present. I would drop my eraser on the floor so that when I bent over to pick it up I could get a quick look under the teacher's desk and see between her legs. If I was lucky, I might even get a peek at her panties. She knew I did that. All the guys who sat in that middle row did it. And she got off on it. If she hadn't liked it, she would have changed the position of her desk, or she wouldn't have sat there.

Once a week we had a music class. A lady violinist came around to teach that class. She was beautiful and she could make her violin laugh and cry and talk and sing. I can still hear all those beautiful things she played, and I can still remember how horny she made me. All that is still mixed up inside me, the music, the beautiful woman, the feeling of wanting to do something to her or with her (I could scarcely imagine what or how), and the beautiful, horny hurt of seeing her go away, knowing I wouldn't see her again for a whole week. Now what kind of a musical education was that? All I can say is, that was the one part of my school experience which was vibrantly alive. It crackled with meaning. And I learned to love music, to love the classics she played. That love she instilled has carried me on into an exploration of music which has never stopped.

More than any other kind of nourishment, kids need love. Without it they'll shrivel up and die, they know that instinctively. So it is not surprising that love is what they want most to know about. Love is the focal point of their curiosity. And they want to know about the mechanics of love—physics, biology, chemistry. We teach these subjects, but we don't abandon ourselves to them. We even call them disciplines. We learn, knowing not what we learn, because none of it is within a love context. We are aware of no encompassing principle. For classroom purposes we take the glowing stuff of life and sterilize it. All our organized knowledge is sexless and lifeless. That's what I mean about that lady with her violin. She brought sex and love and life into that classroom, loads of it. She created a sea of love for all us kids to swim in. I almost drowned in it.

I am opposed to schools and schooling. I keep saying in public that we should burn the schools. There is nothing vindictive in that statement; it is just that I know the schools stand in the way of life and learning. The only justification for not burning them would be that they exist to satisfy the natural curiosity of children. But that's not what school is all about. If it was, the educators wouldn't be trying to design sex-education courses for the kids; they would realize that sex is already in the school. Every classroom is full of it. There might also be some realization that the entire universe is sexual—made up of a vast array of polarities—and that what we call nature is the composite result of never-ending intercourse between those polarities. Excluding love and sex from learning is like trying to exclude food and drink from living. But our attempts to do so have been so successful that now, for many, they subsist only as pornography.

Meantime, I have two kids who attend school: Jennifer, who is in her early teens and about to enter high school, and Gregory, who is much younger. They go to school because that's their choice. It isn't mine. I think the attraction is social. I hope there may be some things there that turn them on, just as there were some things for me. My concern is not that they learn, not that they get an education, but only that they don't suffer any crippling damage. So far, I'm not too anxious about it because they don't seem to be taking it seriously.

I know quite a few adults who have an enduring hatred for school. They're very bitter about it, and I think that's because school made them feel dumb. A real putdown. And maybe I escaped that because I wasn't able to take it seriously. Because I really was dumb—I believed that. Even before I started school, people all said, "Wilfred's not ready for school yet." And I guess I wasn't ready, either. So they held me back a year. And I really wanted to go to school. That's how dumb I was!

I was so dumb! they'd ask me a question and it would be just like . . . well, it was no use asking me anything in school. I can remember many times I knew the answers to questions but refused to say them. In class, the teacher would ask me something: "Wilfred, do you know this?" And even if I knew it I wouldn't get up and say it, because I was sort of guessing. The other kids—the white kids—didn't know either, but they would try to bluff it out, make half a dozen guesses. I could never do that. I had to be absolutely sure or I wouldn't say anything.

There was only one exception to that in all my time in school, only once when I wasn't dumb. That was when I dreamed about "The Walrus and the Carpenter." It was memory work we were supposed to do, two verses of "The Walrus and the Carpenter." I had read that poem through a number of times and I liked it. And now I was lying on my bed trying to memorize two verses. I was really concentrating. Then after a while my aunt Lou came and lay down with me and tried to help me. She said, "What have you got to do?" and I said, "I've got to memorize two verses of this poem and say them in school tomorrow." Then she took the book and tried to get me to recite, but I couldn't remember anything. So she told me the first two lines and I repeated them after her; then the next two and the next, over and over until I thought I knew it. "Okay," she said, "that's the first verse, now let's do the next one. Only six more lines." So we did that one. Then she came back to the first verse, and I couldn't remember a thing, just no way. Finally, I gave the whole thing up. I said, "I just can't do it." Then we turned out the lights and went to sleep.

When I woke up in the morning I sat right up in bed, and I remembered dreaming that I knew that poem by heart, not just two verses but the whole thing, and that I had recited it in school. I sat there in bed, and to my own amazement, I reeled off the whole poem right to the end.

At school that day different kids got up and recited two verses. And some recited three and some recited four and five, and the teacher thought that was great. Then my turn came and I recited the two perfectly. That surprised her because I couldn't remember two lines any other time. Then—I don't know why—she said, "Do you know any more?" and I said, "Yes, teacher," and I said the next verse. "Do you know any more?" "Yeah." "Next verse . . ." Then she asked me, "How many verses do you know?" And I said, "I know all of them, teacher." Well, that blew her mind. That teacher just sat there, befuddled. Finally she said, "Well, it just couldn't be—well, say it, then." So I went through it and I think there was something like eighteen verses in that poem. I said them all right through to the finish, and then she wouldn't believe it. She thought I must be cheating, and I don't blame her. She couldn't find a way out of it—I had recited the whole damn thing. She looked for pieces of paper. She came down to my desk while I was reciting, to see if I had a book open; she really gave all the other kids close around me the once-over. Then she just shook her head.

I don't know what to make of that experience except that maybe we could learn everything in that same effortless way if we weren't conditioned to do things through hard work and striving. Another time, later in life, I experienced going inside a cuckoo clock and afterward I could remember everything about that clock, how it was put together inside. I just became very small or the clock became big, and I wandered around on the wheels and springs and screws.

A long time later I discovered that one of the most important ways of learning used by my people in the old days was dreams. And today, that's coming back in some Indian communities. People go away, go out in the bush and fast, and after a few days and nights they begin dreaming. They learn all kinds of practical things from those dreams. And they bring that back to the people.

I imagine that in the old tribal days everyone must have sensed that people are born knowing how to be humans, just as beavers are born knowing how to be beavers, and that learning is an aspect of normal human behavior —built in. So there wouldn't have been any more concern about children learning than there would have been about them breathing or eating. There may have been times when children were instructed, individually and informally and in circumstances that seemed to justify adult interference. But I am sure when that occurred, it was always associated with a skill or a technique—with doing, never with being. To those people, teaching behavior to a child would have been as stupid as teaching a beaver to build dams.

2·The Parasites

I BELIEVE Western European culture will never endure in the Americas. I believe it is only a passing phase like the hoola hoop or the skate board. I also believe that the peoples living in the Americas will become American; that they will have to in order to survive in America. That means that a truly *American* culture will evolve—is evolving—in the Americas, a culture which is not a European import, nor an adaptation of a European import. That means that the sons and daughters of immigrants who strove for over four-hundred years to possess the Americas will be possessed by the Americas; the descendants of those who tried to conquer and subdue the Americas will be conquered and subdued by the Americas. It means that the stubborn land the pioneers cleared and cursed will be loved, respected, and revered by the great-grandchildren of pioneers. And the native creatures of that land will also be loved and fostered, including the original American human: the Indian.

That is faith. My faith. It is not the faith of the church. It is faith in life, not afterlife. It is also optimism. But I am not optimistic about civilization. I am optimistic about people and about life.

[55]

Life is sacred. And life is happening, miraculously, every day, not just on Sundays. People are sacred, people are miracles, and they too are happening every day. For me, all that adds up to religion, a religion that is a total way of life. Whole. Holy. It means that the part of life the Christians call secular is a cop-out and a mockery.

Last summer in the Alberta foothills, there was an Indian Ecumenical Conference. It took a lot of effort and money for that to happen, but there they were, 130-odd Indian religious leaders from every part of North America. Medicine men and some Indian clergy. After nearly five hundred years of persecution, the old-way-of-life religions were still very much alive.

For me, that conference meant many things. But there was one thing about it that was very personal: I had the feeling that I had come full circle and had finally made it. It felt like at last I was back home.

You see, I was born in the church, the Holy Christian, Catholic Church. I never had a chance to go to it; it came to me. Its representatives had invaded my community and set up their establishment a hundred years before I was born. There were no Mohammedan missionaries around there, selflessly dedicated to converting us savages, or Buddhists or Hindus. And that is something to think about.

When I started school on the reserve I got far more religion than education. We spent more time learning the catechism than we ever spent with spelling or arithmetic. Attending Mass was a big part of school. We went as a class, and when we got in the church all the boys were put on one side in the front pews and all the girls on the other. There was one of those sisters or whatever she was—a schoolteacher—with a little clapper board. This thing would come down and make a noise; then we would stand. Next time she clapped it, everybody would sit or kneel or something. We all went by this little clapper like a bunch of trained seals. So that's how we sort of functioned in there.

You know, we played around like all kids—most of us. We didn't pray. I had no idea what was going on in church, I was just there. What interested me about church, mostly, was to be an altar boy. To go up there and work with the priest. I guess it seemed to me that's where the action was. I remember wanting to do that, but I could never make it. I finally got to wear a cassock—you know, those big long gowns. I never did get to participate in anything more than just carrying that candle, but I watched. I really watched everything that was being done, and memorized the whole complicated sequence of the Mass. But I had no idea what it all meant. That's not where my interest was. I wanted to participate in the ritual. As I grew older I guess I realized I'd never be able to do that. Then I felt the priests were having all the fun and the people were having something done to them rather than being included as participants.

In later years, when I began to have some experience of Indian religious practices, I realized that my childhood feelings about the Mass had been essentially correct. I have never participated in an Indian religious ceremony that did not include everyone present as an *active* participant. Indian religious leaders are not trained as priests. They are just people who feel moved to perform a ritual which *others recognize* as having a deep religious significance. *That* is their qualification, that recognition. But they're just people in the community. No titles, no special way of dressing. They're just John or Henry or Fred. (Our doctors are the same.) The church may survive, but it will only do so by recognizing that we are all equal before God; by recognizing that any person who feels moved to do so should be free to conduct Mass or perform a religious service—and do that *in his own way*. There is no other valid qualification.

A few months ago I attended the funeral of one of my relatives. The church where the Mass was said was in a big American city. The three priests who conducted the Mass were very old men, and it soon became apparent that they were senile. The priest who was saying the Mass was silent for long periods, as if trying to remember what came next. Then he would go on, and he wasn't able to remember because the Mass didn't follow the usual routine. When he wasn't able to find the proper passages in the Bible, he read others or just used his own words. And to me, his words were beautiful because they seemed to be coming from his heart rather than a book. The other two priests who were serving got mixed up with the incense and sometimes didn't seem to know when to kneel and when to stand. But those in attendance weren't disturbed by any of this. Many of them hadn't been to church in a long time and didn't, themselves, remember the routine too well. The result was that people were standing and kneeling as they felt moved to do so, rather than according to any set procedure. And it all felt good. It felt like everyone was participating instead of being processed through a mechanical kind of thing.

After we moved off the reserve and went to Ten Mile Point, a priest used to come through. He used to travel to different communities on Sunday and have Mass somewhere at nine, and then again at eleven someplace else. He had to drive between these communities. So I traveled with him for a while. And that's how I finally got the chance to serve Mass. The priest got caught in a situation where there was no one except me, and he called me over and asked, "Can you serve Mass?" and I said, "Yes, father." And I knew that he didn't believe me because I also knew he'd been to Wikwemikong. He used to go over there and he must have known I'd never served Mass. When I said yes, I meant that I knew how to serve Mass, not that I'd done it. So I served Mass right there. I did the whole thing and he didn't have to tell me anything.

I was curious about him because he was a drunk. But that's not really a fair statement. I think he got to be an alcoholic later, I'm not sure. But anyway, he used to drink a lot. Ten Mile Point was unorganized territory and we were under a prohibition act or something, so there were all kinds of bootleggers, and we used to serve booze at the lodge. And sometimes in winter he'd get stuck between towns. His car would be stuck there all night and he couldn't get through. So he'd stop and drink; throw off a bottle of whiskey in an evening. That was a good relationship because—well, a priest was like a god to me, but this was the only priest who was not like that. He was human and he treated me like a human being. But the rest of them, no matter who they were, always pushed us down. I guess when I got older I began to understand that all clergymen are hypocrites.

When I was a child I regarded the priests as more than human. They stood somewhere between me and God, and considerably closer to God than to me. And they were responsible for that image, not me. Then as I got older I began to discover they were just as human as anyone else and sometimes they did things that even I wouldn't do, like carrying stories and gossiping and prying into people's private affairs. I knew they did that because they would come right out with it in church, naming names and everything. The only other place they could have got that information was in the confessional. Like most clergy they considered visiting an important part of their job, so they spent a lot of time visiting around the community and talking with people. That's where they picked up all that garbage.

Anyhow, I hung on to that religion even though I got to believe in it less and less. It was really contradictory; the priests weren't practicing all the things they said. I'd hear them say something, but in practice that's not what they'd do. I got to really question that. Then there were those other religions, and I thought, Well, that's funny, people belong to these others and ours is supposed to have everything. How come they don't know that? There were all the Protestant people, you see, and my religion made me look down on them. Catholicism is the one and only true religion: that's what I was taught. Then I began to find there were lots of people of various faiths who also thought theirs was the only true religion. So I began to wonder how there could be several one and only true religions, all of them Christian.

Of course, I had that whole thing about heaven and hell; all that stuff had been drilled into me in school. I knew I was being mistreated by priests and nuns, but it was a bind because at the same time I thought one of the worst things was to be a person who wasn't a Catholic. They used to talk about Indians not being Christians in the old days, and I used to think, Holy God, that must have been awful because look what you got to go through to be a Christian. My people must have been bad; they were all savages. But all those ideas came from the church.

I never stopped to think at the time that I was happiest when I was just there with that community and being that savage, heathen, or whatever it was they saw us as.

Then my oldest brother, Eugene, was always talking about other religions, Buddhism and Hinduism and all kinds of others. But I couldn't picture any of that because all I knew was the Catholic religion. Even though Eugene told me about those things, they didn't have any meaning. Then one night old Ike came into the lodge to get boozed up.

Old Ike was not a regular patron; sometimes we wouldn't see him for months. But everybody knew him. He was a bum and an alcoholic, but we were always glad to see him because even though he was a terrible liar, the stories he told were great. I don't know what his last name was; he was just old Ike and he came from down Shaguiandah way. That's about all I knew about him.

There weren't many people staying in the lodge that night—maybe half a dozen because it was winter—and they all sat together down at one end of the lounge. And old Ike sat with them. Well, after a while they began talking about religion. Old Ike just listened at first, then he beckoned and asked me to bring him a cigar—a sure sign he was about ready to do some talking. I brought him a White Owl and stayed right there to listen. Sure enough, after he'd fired up his stogy, he leaned back in his chair and cleared his throat.

"I'm a Catholic," he said, "and I consider myself a good Catholic, even though I never go near a church no more." He took a big drag on his cigar and waited for that opening statement to sink in. "In other words, I reserve the right to interpret what's a good Catholic and what ain't. And I'll tell you why I feel that way about it.

"I was born a Catholic, and when I was just a little tad those priests scairt the daylights outa me. They had me so scairt with stories about hellfire and the devil and all that I was a-scairt to go out if it was dark. Wouldn't even go to the outhouse. Well, when I growed up a little and got in my teens I begun to resent all that. You know how a young feller is? Sort of rebellious. And I seen, too, the priests themselves wasn't all that holy. So I got to thinkin'. And I thought, 'Why are they always telling us we mustn't read the Bible for ourselves? Mustn't even own one. Why do they say, if we got any questions about the Holy Scripture we should ask them?' And do you know what conclusion I come to?" Old Ike looked around at his listeners and tapped the ash off his cigar. "They must be hiding somethin'. Yes sir, that's what I thought. There must be things in that book they don't want us to know. So you know what I done? I got me a Bible. Yes sir, stole it out of a hotel room. A Gideon."

At this point old Ike asked me to bring him another beer, and filled with admiration for his daring and fear for his soul, I hurried to get it. Stealing a Bible! That was pretty bad.

"Well, you know I was right?" Old Ike was saying. "That Bible was just full of things those priests had never mentioned. Like Samson and Delilah, for instance. You got any idea what those two were really up to? And Solomon—all I ever heard was how wise he was. But he was a regular four-peckered billy goat. Had more concubines than he had brains—lots more. And even our Lord, you know, He had His moments. If I hadn't of read that Bible I just never would have got no clear idea about Him, not at all. The way them priests talked about Him, I had this picture . . . well, He was almost like a ghost, floatin' around two, three feet off the ground. Not real. Just not real at all. But I found out He was a regular guy. Real down to earth. And nothin' uppity about him, neither. Just plain folks."

"Did you read the whole thing, Ike?" one of the other men asked. "Cover to cover?"

"No," said old Ike. "You see, I had to keep it hid under my mattress and could only read at night after I went to bed. I just hunted through it for the juicy parts—skipped all the begats and stuff like that. But I read all the New Testament more than once. And you know what's my favorite part? The wedding feast. Turning the water into wine. Now, there's an example of real religion and real love." He emptied his glass and wiped his mouth on his sleeve.

"There's this big wedding, see. All kinds of guests. And after the wedding there's a party, naturally. Just when the party is goin' good, everybody dancin' and singin' and whoopin' her up, you know what happens?" Old Ike paused for dramatic effect. "They run out of booze.

"Can't you just picture it? The party is just nicely under way and now it's going to die on its feet. The hostess is all upset, the liquor stores are all closed, and the local bootlegger is sold out. What are they going to do? But our Lord is there, see. He's a guest too. And He steps up to the hostess, real quiet and easy, and He says, Got any water? And she says, Sure, lots of it, but what good is that? And He says, Never mind. Just bring me a tubful of it. So they do that and He just makes a pass or two over it, and presto! it turns into wine."

Old Ike sat back, smiling triumphantly. "Now that's what I call a miracle!" he said, as if he had just performed it himself.

When I heard that old man talking that way and all those guys laughing, I was scared, I really was. I wasn't standing over there near them any more. No sir. Any moment, I expected a bolt of lightning to come sizzling down through the roof and strike old Ike dead. But nothing happened. Old Ike just went on talking.

"Must have been a real party man, our Lord. I bet every hostess in the country was after Him. But you know, it wasn't the miracle that was important. That's where the church misses the whole point. It was that He came through in the clutch. It wouldn't have mattered even if He'd had some booze hid out somewheres and brought it in just when they needed it. I mean, that would have been miracle enough. The point is, He saved the party.

"So that's why I say I'm a good Catholic even though I don't go to church. Because I found out I'm a lot more like our Lord than any of those damned priests. I found out He liked parties. Well, I like parties. He liked booze. I like booze. He didn't get along with the church and the priests. Neither do I. He had no visible means of support. Neither do I. He was a shit-disturber. So am I. He liked little kids. So do I. He hung around with prostitutes and other outcasts. So do I."

That whole thing was a shock to me. It really shook me up, but it was the best thing that could have happened—better than all the Sunday School lessons in the world. Old Ike was right. Jesus Christ, as the church presented Him, was unreal. And old Ike had turned Him into flesh and blood.

Shortly after that we moved from Ten Mile Point to Sault Sainte Marie, where there were lots of Protestants, and I didn't find any of the bad things in those people I had been taught to expect. Working in the city, rubbing shoulders with all kinds of people, it really hit me that that whole church thing was a big con job of some kind. And it was all about making money. The whole thing was money, money, money. I could see that the church was really just a big manufacturing company. Their product was salvation, manufactured from the raw material in the Bible. In addition to various services, they sold forgiveness of sins, absolution, and one-way tickets to heaven. You even had to pay for a place to sit in the church, and when they got you in there that damned basket never stopped coming around: collections for the missions, for lost souls, for some church they wanted to build someplace. There was no end to it. That was when I turned the whole thing down and quit. That was it. I said to hell with it, I ain't going back to church no more.

It's funny how I defined religion in those days. Religion was the church and the church, religion—especially the Catholic church. It took me a long time to remember that my people had a religion and to start feeling my way back to that. When I was just a little boy I had seen medicine men do lots of strange things; they used to shake rattles or something they'd bring, and they'd burn things, and I didn't know what all that was about. I had no idea. But the Catholic priests would also come when there was a death or a funeral or if there was sickness. The medicine people (they could be men or women) came only when they were asked to come. But if they were asked, they couldn't refuse, and of course, the priest had to come because it was his duty. So it was a whole double-barreled thing. The Indians weren't going to lose out: they'd get the medicine people *and* the priests. Why take a chance? The priest must never see the medicine man, because if

the priest knew they were using "medicine" when somebody was sick, that was it. He wouldn't come at all. He'd
say they were practicing Indian religion. And anyone
who didn't go to church couldn't be buried in church
grounds. Until recently, if a person died from drunken-
ness or something, it didn't matter whether it happened
to be the first time he'd gotten drunk in his life and he'd
been the best guy that ever lived up to that moment, they
wouldn't bury him in consecrated ground. You had to die
respectable.

I'd see the medicine men any other time in our community and we were friends, but when they came to do
those ceremonies I was scared. Or I think I was scared;
maybe it was something that made me sort of respect
them. I just moved out of the way. A priest came there and
he did his services and got all the people going; they'd all
pray and all that and that didn't bother me. But the medicine men frightened me. Maybe I was picking up the
feelings of the older people.

The church called the Indian ceremonies superstition
and forbade them, so the ceremonies were driven under-
ground. Those priests with their robes on and big authority would walk right into homes and just give hell to
everybody. They'd say, "You're practicing witchcraft," to
the people in those homes. The people wouldn't be doing
anything; they were just there. Maybe somebody'd be
boiling up some herbs for a medicine and they'd say,
"Those are superstitions you've got; that's nothing but
witchcraft and it's bad to practice that." And people got
very disturbed about it.

I guess what really sort of staggers me when I look
back on all that now is the arrogant assumption of those
priests that everyone is inherently bad and sinful. And

superstition! Those priests were the most superstitious people I ever knew except for us kids. Kids are more superstitious than anyone. Cut your hand between the finger and thumb and wham! you've got lockjaw. Pick up a toad—you got warts. If the moon shone on your face while you were sleeping you'd wake up with your mouth all twisted. One time my grandfather told us that if we made fun of a cripple we'd lose our eyesight, and I believed that. Later on I decided it was just another superstition. Now I suspect he meant that if all you can see in a cripple is something to laugh at, your eyesight is perceptive but not visionary.

I went to Communion and leaving the church afterward I'd feel really good—pure. I'd go straight home so as not to become involved with the guys who hadn't taken Communion that Sunday—the unwashed. If someone offered me a drag on a cigarette, I'd refuse. But I could never maintain that sanctity for very long. It just didn't become me. A couple of hours after Mass I'd be out in the bushes somewhere studying anatomy with some little girl or into some other delicious bag of sins. My problem was that most of the time I just felt so damn good, happy and joyful, that I couldn't get serious about sin. I couldn't get serious about God either. I didn't know Him, had never seen Him. I didn't know anything about all that God business. Sometimes I'd be told, "Go pray to Saint Ann," or pray to this one or that one. And I'd go into the church and kneel in front of the statue, looking around all the time to see if someone was looking, because I really felt very foolish. That was a bad trip for me, but I'd go and do it just the same.

There were times when I knew I really felt good about being in church. Maybe it was the organ or a song or those stained windows. But it was also hard to feel good coming out of that church.

I didn't know until I went to church off the reserve that there were sermons about the gospel. At Wikwemikong they'd take the Bible and they'd open it up and read us a thing, and then they'd talk about that, very briefly. Maybe a bit about getting along together or loving thy neighbor or something. Then they'd drop all that religious stuff and get down to the nitty-gritty: the behavior of the community. They'd say, "Well, Edith got drunk again last night and so did George. And there was a big fight. The fights in this community have got to stop." And for the next hour the people would catch hell, just like a bunch of little kids. And a lot of culprits would be named and called down in public. Until I got outside that community I never once heard a sermon about the Bible. All the sermons were tirades about behavior or instructions, like, Send your children to the dentist and get their teeth fixed—You shouldn't be giving them candy, it's bad for the teeth—Now, all the boys were playing up the hill last week; they shouldn't be playing there, they should be down by the school—and on and on and on. Today the subject matter is changed—they complain about cars roaring around the community—but it's still going on. Religion, where I grew up, was pretty weird.

But sometimes the people used to sort of get back at the priests. In the old days and even occasionally in recent times some ambitious priest would decide he was going to preach in the Indian language. Well, he'd try that and sure as hell he'd screw up everything, all the words. He'd talk along, not saying what he thought he was saying at all. The people would sit through it having a terrible time to keep from laughing, and afterwards they'd go and home and they'd say, "This is what he said . . ." and they'd repeat it. Then they'd laugh like hell. That would keep them entertained for a long time.

To me, one of the saddest things about priests, and all clergy for that matter, is that they're all a bunch of bums. Maybe that is a sort of vocational conditioning they all suffer from. I could never understand that: why they go around bumming, even from the poorest person in the community. Give, give, give to the church. It always seemed to me that if the church was really turning people on (which is what religion is all about) the clergy would never have to beg for support. They'd be flooded with it. They'd also see that money is the least of it. Instead they're pushing a product and they have to use bribes and threats to get people to buy it.

And confession. What a thing that was. I never told the truth in any confession I ever went to that I can remember. But it wasn't because I was trying to conceal something; it was because I didn't know what was sin and what wasn't. I couldn't figure that out because the things I enjoyed always seemed to be the things that I shouldn't do, and I wouldn't talk about that. Maybe I just never could believe pleasure is bad. So I'd make up stuff, because they taught us how to go to confession. You're supposed to go there and say, "I'm sorry, father, that I have sinned . . ." and then you say the act of contrition. And after that's over, then you're supposed to say, "Well, I stole an apple" or "I stole this or that." There was no such a thing as stealing in our community because we were a sharing society. Nobody owned anything, so you couldn't steal. I'd think, Well, I got to go to confession, so what can I make up? and I'd think about it, and when I'd get there I'd just say a bunch of things. "Well, I didn't listen to my

parents five times," I'd say, and silly things like that. So
he'd give me penance. Anytime I did something really
wrong, I'd never tell him; he'd be the last guy I'd tell. You
know, I sometimes sat there in the church doing my penance, and I'd just sit there and confess my sins sort of to
myself, or else it seemed like I was saying, "Well, Jesus or
God, I'm sorry. I'll try to be better in the future, I'll try
to change my ways." That to me was a more meaningful
confession. I couldn't tell that guy over there anything.
He knew everybody in the community, he knew everybody's voice, and he could see, anyway, through that
damned thing. Hell, I just made stuff up. I'm not the only
one—all the kids I knew did that. You ask most of them;
they'll all tell you the same thing. We even used to talk
about that when we got together: "What did you tell?"
Then somebody . . . you know, they'd make it up, maybe
even make the story bigger. "Ahhh," they'd say, "You
never said that—did you really say that?" "Yeah, I said
that." And then we'd all laugh like hell. And then somebody else would say, "This is what I told him last week."
All they were doing was telling the priest a bunch of lies.
Going to confession and telling a whole bunch of lies.

Well, all that is long gone, back there on the other side
of my life. One thing about growing up in an Indian
community is it gives you insights into white behavior
and white culture that few whites ever have. You know,
you grow up there among your own people, then one day
you leave. You go out there into the white world and all
that seems very strange. People behave very differently,
and that really sharpens you up. You get very observant
because you want to learn how to do everything right. But
you also become very conscious of your Indianness, of
being different, of how different the people are back

home. And you begin to ask yourself why that is and which is right, and you get into a big conflict about all that. Then one day you go home—back to the reserve—and boy! that's when it really hits you. It happened to me. I came home one time and my people were all gone. There was nobody there any more—no people. Only Indians. *That* is when I knew I was Indian, that's when I really knew. And there was no way back to my people. I could only go ahead.

But I found my people again. It took a long time, but I found them. And not just Indian people. I found humans. And some of them are white.

3·One of the Strangers

MOVING TO Sault Sainte Marie was my introduction to urban life. The Sault was not a big city, but it seemed like a big town to me. There were even trolley cars running on tracks right through the center of town. And of course, lots of automobiles and big stores and people all over the place.

I was fourteen or fifteen at that time and still living at home with my family. My father bought a big old house. And there were a whole lot of people living in that house, not just our family. In the family there were us four boys (Eugene, Earl, Thomas, Jr., and I) and two girls (Rosemary and Yvonne), and my father and mother. Then there were some friends of ours, the Fitzpatricks, and they had two children. In the winter there was Stan and Don Fisher, who were from Wikwemikong, and my friend Dolph Lewis always lived with us, and Wanley. And sometimes my cousin Victor would stay with us for a while, or Herman, or both of them. So it was quite a large household. Practically all of us were young people, all living together in that house, and we were full of energy and always up to something.

We had a newspaper; it was called *The Tatler*. We named it *The Tatler* because that's what it was all about— it was a means for people in the house to tattle on each other. We had a typewriter in the house, and each person had a by-line. The paper never really "came out." It's more accurate to say that it was continually in motion; it was coming out all the time. Whenever anyone had something to tattle about or got an inspiration, they would go to the typewriter and get out some little item for the newspaper under their particular by-line. Nothing appeared in that paper anonymously: that was a sort of unwritten rule, a point of honor for all tattlers.

The items in it were mostly about the activities of all those people. Of course, all of us had some desire to have a private life, but that was very difficult because there would be items like "Who came in at two o'clock in the morning?" Sometimes we'd hear the girls talking in one of their rooms and we'd eavesdrop and then print everything they said. The whole thing was a kind of communication about things that each one tried to do without anyone else knowing. And sometimes there would be several versions of the same incident in the newspaper, and none of them would be the same.

We had another section that was called "Jokes by Wanley." I don't know how he did it, but every day he would come out with two or three new jokes, and they'd be in that paper. And then there was another section called "Around the Town"; it was written by" Edigee." We had lots of friends around the town, the bunch of us that went around together. There were probably forty people, and they would drop in all the time. They would always want to see the paper, because there were things about them in it.

We had a big dining room in that house, a long narrow room that wasn't heated. We only used it as a dining room on special occasions because it was a lot of trouble to heat it up. The rest of the time it was the ping-pong tournament room. There was a big oak table in there. The boys made a ping-pong table that sat on top of that table, and we had ping-pong games in there all the time. So we had a "rec" room in that old house, and it all happened because there was no heat in the dining room. We had a dart board too—it hung on the back of one of the doors. We put it up one time when my mother was away, and when she came back, the back of that door was all full of little pinholes. She was pretty upset about that. We had to go and get a piece of quarter-ply and hang it up behind the dart board.

Those ping-pong tournaments made us quite famous. They attracted all sorts of people from all over the town. We even had the ping-pong champion of Austria there at one time—at least he *said* he was the ping-pong champion of Austria, and he was a very good player. But Scotty beat him. And the tournaments were all for money—we played for money. Everybody put some in the pot, and whoever won would take the money. Then we'd all go and have a big celebration, a big bash.

When I think back on all that now, I realize how much that town has changed. We used to have sleigh-ride parties in the winter, and you know, we lived right downtown and the sleigh would come right to the front door. Then we'd all get in the sleigh and go out to what we called the twelve-mile block. It was a long ride, three or four hours, and we'd end up back at the house. Then we would eat. My mother would have great big pots of food all cooked, all hot, for when we got back: beans, fresh baked bread, stew, soup. And was it good! There were—oh, usually thirty-five, forty, forty-five people on those sleigh rides. That's all a thing of the past now; you couldn't possibly do it today. For one thing, the snow-clearing facilities are such that there's no snow on the streets downtown.

Our parties, including the sleigh-ride parties, were always filled with music, all kinds of singing. All of us and various other people played musical instruments, so we had lots of music. We would often put on impromptu little shows, little skits and so on. Sometimes we would even persuade my old grandmother to get all dressed up, and she would come out and do a little stepdance or something. What an old character she was! I don't know how many petticoats she wore, but I remember that one of them, at least, always had to be red flannel. I don't remember ever seeing her in any clothes that didn't come right down to her ankles. She always wore high boots, and she smoked a pipe. She would sit in her rocking chair and talk and smoke her pipe. She was a funny but very wonderful old lady. Her eyesight failed in her later years, and sometimes she didn't seem to be able to see very much at all. Other times she could see exceptionally well. At those times when she didn't seem to be able to see she would say, "Oh, I can't see you, but I know you from your voice." But then she would look out the front window, and it seemed to me she could always see everything going on in the street. For instance, she could always see my cousin Alphonse going into the pub across the street. And any members of the household who were leaving the house or coming back, she could always see them and she knew who they were. That was a whole game, I guess, that she played, and of course, we went along. We played it with her.

I found many things different in the city, very different. Being Indian was different. Indians were drunks and bums—it seems everybody knew that. And I was one of those. There was that same idea back at Ten Mile Point and in Little Current, but the lines weren't so sharply drawn. Here there were no exceptions, no acceptable Indians: that was the feeling.

And the whole girl thing was very different. One of the first things I learned was that you related to girls in a way that was almost opposite to the reserve. The guys were after girls. You went out to pick up a girl, and if you were successful that could get you into a whole thing: taking them here and there, dating them, a big game of working up to the point where you made out with them. That had never happened to me before. I didn't know anything about it and it just blew my mind, because back there in my own community no boy ever thought about how to get a girl. On the reserve the boys were there and the girls were there, and the fact that they lived in the same community meant they were together. You just went wherever you were going and there were always girls there. Everybody was completely relaxed about it because it always just worked out. You always seemed to end up with whoever you wanted and you did whatever the two of you wanted to do. Just be together or screw or whatever it was you were up to. It all just happened.

So I discovered that my introduction to sex had been very different on the reserve from what it might have been had I grown up in a white community. I have the impression that in white society, at least for those of my generation, sex and relating to girls was really rough. It was sinful and immoral, stuff like that. There was a whole ritualistic courtship attached to it, and "honorable" intentions. And all that seemed hypocritical and dishonorable to me, because there was no trust there, only anxiety and fear. The girls were afraid of getting knocked up and the boys were afraid of being found out. It also seemed to me that screwing always had to be tied to what I would call romance, which pretty well removed the chance of a young boy being introduced to sex by an older woman.

But there is just no substitute for experience. My own introduction to sex was provided by a relative. I still look on that as one of greatest and happiest experiences of my life. From that time on, it seems to me that I screwed all the time, without letup. Not just my relatives, who were not always available, but anywhere I could find it, and it always seemed to be there. I was always running into some girl or some woman, and our relationship was a sex relationship. That doesn't mean that that's all we did. These were people I had a social relationship with. I saw them lots of places and we did all kinds of things together, but during that period in my life the thing that was foremost, always in my blood and in my brain, was sex.

And you know, that wasn't just a woman thing either. That whole sex thing as I think of it now involved all kinds of people. All the young guys my own age were into it just like I was. But I don't think we talked about sex the same way they do in white society. I don't recall any of those young guys bragging about it, but there was some communication just the same. You always knew what was going on. You had a sort of over-all picture of the sexual activity in that community.

White society, I know, tends to look on sex with one's blood relations as unnatural. But to me it seems the most natural thing in the world. When I think of my cousins now, who introduced my brothers also into sex, I think of them as very kindly, loving people who did something for me which was beautiful and natural. I guess people were honest about their feelings and their needs, and as all the resources of that community were available to those who needed them, sex was not excluded. Sex was a recognized need, so nobody went without it. It was as simple as that.

Maybe I was too old to change by that time. Anyhow, I didn't change; didn't throw away that Indian way of relating to women; didn't try to adopt the white way. When I went to parties, sometimes I took a girl; I guess I usually took a girl, but not always. And I took her to the party, that's all. And I can't recall having any anxiety or any plans about making that girl or making any girl. If it happened, it happened. And often it did happen that I ended up with some girl and balled her. But if that didn't happen I was seldom disappointed, because I didn't have any of those anxious expectations that I could see—that were so painfully evident—in most of the young white guys I knew.

Like most practices in white society, this way of relating between the sexes struck me as very hypocritical. Because the truth was that the girls *did* chase the boys. But a whole ritual had been devised to make it look otherwise; to make it look as if the girls were hard to get; to make it look as if the boys were chasing the girls. So it was really a big moral mess. That's what I mean when I say it was hypocritical. Most of the white boys and girls I knew managed to make out together in spite of that mess, but it was a terrible struggle for them and they had real guilt feelings about it. The girls all played a game called "hard to get," and no girl wanted to become known as an easy piece. The boys played their version of this same game: it was called "nice guy." What that meant was that no nice guy would do a dirty thing like that to a girl unless she was a whore.

We had sex games on the reserve too, but there was no hypocrisy about them. They were teasing games. The girls usually started it. It was letting the guy know they wanted to be screwed, that's what it really was. Mocking him about his manhood, really bugging him. And this was always done openly, in front of everyone, like at a party. And the girl's parents would be right there; the guy's too. All the old folk. And those damned girls could really work that, really try to embarrass a guy in front of everybody. Of course, the whole thing for him, the whole challenge, was not to blow his cool. Just ignore the girl; go right on talking and drinking with the men. But later on he'd get that girl and really put it to her. So everybody knew about that. Took it for granted. And those people on the reserve would have been shocked, just as I was, to discover that out there in white society nice people waited until they were married and only bad people, people with no morals and no character, did it out of wedlock. And if you never got married you just never got screwed. No way.

I guess that's a whole Christian hang-up. But it must be a white peculiarity too, because on the reserve we were all good Catholics and the priests never stopped lecturing us about sex; telling us it was sinful, that even for married people it was wrong to do it for pleasure; that it should only be done for procreation. But nobody I know of ever paid any attention to that. I guess everyone just sort of wrote it off as foolishness. There were lots of things the priests just had no idea about. And how could they know anything about sex? They weren't into that themselves, were they?

Another thing I found pretty different was school. People took it seriously. Everybody: kids and adults. And the schools were big, hundreds of kids and big buildings that cost thousands of dollars. Maybe that's why it was all so serious. Well, I went around to the technical school. They asked me what grade I was in, and I said nine. So they wanted to see my certificate for passing out of grade eight. Well, that really shocked me. I didn't have any certificate. Grade eight was just the last grade I'd been in. As a matter of fact, I don't think I ever passed out of any grade. I just got older and bigger. But anyway, they let me into grade nine.

But I couldn't hack it. This was an institution, my first experience of an institution. With all those hundreds of strangers hurrying here and there and bells ringing all over the place, it was like being in a big railroad station and running on schedule. Too much for me. And you know, students are second-class citizens. Well, I was a student *and* an Indian, so that made me third class, and that's pretty far down the social ladder. So I took to my old bad habit of playing hooky.

I found it wasn't so easy to play hooky in the city as it had been in the country. Besides, it was the wrong time of year—November, and cold. I'd start off for school with my lunch and my books, knowing I'd never get there. I'd go downtown and wander around looking in the store windows, trying to put in the time till three in the afternoon. Trying to find a place to get in out of the cold and keep warm. I found out that businesses—stores and restaurants and places like that—are very suspicious if you come in and don't buy something right away; they figure you're a thief or a bum or something. I guess that's how I discovered the pool hall.

I went in this cigar store one morning around ten, maybe ten thirty, I guess, just to get warm. I stood around looking out the window, and after a while the guy says, "Did you want something, son?" So I said, "No, I guess not," and started for the door. Then he says, "If you're looking for the pool hall, it's in back." Well, it was real cold that morning, so I went around the end of the counter and I went in there.

It was a big room and pretty dark. There was an old guy sitting on a high stool behind a counter and a young guy talking to him. When the young guy saw me, he said, "Want to shoot a game, kid?" I said, "No, I ain't got no money." "That's okay," he said, "I'll pay." Then he turned on a big light over one of the tables and took a cue from the rack. As I took off my jacket and mitts, I noticed there was a triangle of colored balls on the table. Then I got a cue. "Okay," he said, "shoot for break." And he poked this white ball with his cue, sort of gentle, down to the end of the table. It bounced off and came back, maybe three inches. He wet his finger and marked where the ball was and rolled it back to me. Well, I tried to do it like I saw him do it, but I guess I was pretty awkward. The ball went down and hit the end and came almost all the way back. "Okay," he says. "You ever played pool before, kid?" And I said, "No, this is my first time." I thought he'd be mad, but he just laughed and said, "Okay, I'll teach you."

Lanky Lindsey, my own special pool teacher! Well, after that I went to school every day—pool school. I had found something I really wanted to learn, and I learned fast. Lanky was good, one of the best in town, but I got so I could beat him pretty regular. I got to be a real pool shark. I went there most days about nine and stayed all day. Sometimes there wouldn't be anyone there that early, but after a while guys would come in and they were always looking for a partner and that was how I'd get to play. But that was only at first. After a while, when I began to make some money at it, then I could play anytime. I learned the afternoons and evenings were the best. That's when the place was crowded, lots of guys there, some of them pretty good. Before long I was winning twenty, twenty-five dollars a week just shooting pool. A pretty good living for a kid, in those times.

Then I discovered the bowling alley. I had a friend, a young guy who set pins over there, and lots of days, especially in the mornings, there would be no one bowling. So he'd get me to come over and I'd set pins for him. Then he'd set pins for me and I'd bowl. Well, I got to be a pretty good bowler, too. They used to give away a turkey, or sometimes ten bucks, for the highest score of the week. I remember one time I brought home a turkey three weeks in a row. Then I missed a couple of weeks and then I got two more. We had a lot of turkey at our house that winter.

What really attracted me to those places, especially the pool hall, was that I was accepted there. That was far more important than the fun I had playing those games. Nobody gave a damn if I was Indian or what I was. I was taken at face value, and later on I was respected as a good player. That felt good. It gave me a little confidence, and I needed that. The people there were not very high up on the social scale, but to me they were the best people in town. And I still feel that way. There was far more warmth and companionship in the pool hall than there was in all the schools and the churches put together. I guess that's always been a worry to clergymen, but they've never figured it out. Their idea of a solution has always been negative: Close the pool halls! At least on Sundays.

They're hung up on buildings, I guess. "Where two or three are gathered together" . . . Now, He didn't say in a church or in a cathedral or anything like that. And He didn't say they had to be praying or singing hymns. You seldom see any of the clergy in the pool hall or the pubs, yet there are always a lot of people there. It has always seemed to me that religion would be a lot more practical if the church went to the people instead of the people going to the church.

But I learned more at pool school than just how to play pool. I learned a little psychology—how to make it look like you were just lucky. A lucky pool player can make a little change at the game, but nobody will play with a shark. How to goof up: miss shots and scratch and stuff like that, and then bear down and "get lucky" when it counts. I took lots of guys that way, and some of them were better players than I was. I learned a little about competition, too. In the long run, competition is always a putdown, a sure way to fail. You can get to be a really good pool player or bowler or whatever, but there is always someone who's better. You can even be a big frog in a small puddle, but that guy who is better will be along. And he'll beat you.

Well, that was the end of my schooling and the beginning of my learning. You learn by doing, and I did lots of things all over the country. I learned a little bit about sawmills and steel mills and smelters and how to build houses and how to pour cement and pick apples and grow potatoes, and lots of other things. I even played semipro baseball for a while. What I learned from that is that it's no fun sitting on the bench. So I got off the bench one day and went home to Sault Sainte Marie.

I went guiding that fall. I didn't know anything about guiding, but I was Indian and guiding is part of the mythology of being Indian. All Indians are supposed to be good guides. But I had shot lots of deer and considered myself a pretty good hunter. Well, I had a lot to learn and if it hadn't been for the other guides at the lodge, especially the older men, I might not be around today. The first thing they told me was that I had to stay alive and also keep the members of my party from getting shot. "Remember," they said, "every one of those guys has a gun and every one of them wants a deer real bad. So they're trigger-happy."

Well, that scared me real bad because while they're telling me this I'm getting my first impression of hunters. They're arriving at the lodge, and that scares me even more. There's this guy arrives with a minnow pail. Along with all his other gear he brings a minnow pail. On a hunting trip! Because he didn't know that that goes with fishing gear. Honest to God! He really brought it. And another guy says, "What did you bring that for? That's a minnow pail, you put minnows in it and go fishing." "Ohhh," he says. He didn't even know. He knew the gun, I guess, and recognized it. But then he goes into a store, I suppose, and I don't know what people sell them in the stores. He might say, well, he's going hunting. "Then you got to have a shirt, this kind of trousers, those kind of boots," a certain kind, see. And a mackinaw all red or checkered or something, and then he's got a cap, he's got that outfit on, and then: "You've got to have a compass and a call. Here's a deer call, here's a moose call. Now, in the fall when you're out there you might even spot ducks, so here, take a duck call along." Then they've got belts to carry the cartridges and they've got a knapsack and they've got all kinds of stuff. Burdened! They're really burdened down. And they've got three boxes of shells in their pockets as a rule. At least!

When I go hunting I take seven, eight shells, maybe. I just put them in my pocket and I get out into the bush and I shove them in the rifle and I always have about three extra shells, or four. Or sometimes if I've got a coat, I can carry the box of shells. Then I may take a box with me. Hell! I can go hunting with two or three shells. I've gone hunting with one—that's all I had.

Well, they had everything. Some of them even had markers for marking the trees so they could tell where they were. I even found out that some of them carried string. You wouldn't believe it—string! So they can tie it to a tree on the road and walk into the bush on the string, letting it out bit by bit till they come to the end of it, and then that's where they sit. Then they pull themselves back out of the bush on this store string—store string, that's all. They follow the string back, rolling it up as they go, and finally they're back on the road. They don't know where they are once they get in there; they totally lose sight of all direction. They just don't know, really! When people are that helpless, it scares you.

Oh, I was scared. Every time I took them out I'd preach to them. "Now look, you guys, don't you *dare* shoot me," I'd say to them. "Look at me, I ain't got no antlers and I walk on only two legs, so just make sure it's a deer before you shoot. Now, if you start wandering around I'm not going to know where you are and I'm going to be in that bush driving deer this way. Now I *know* where you are, so *stay* right here." And I'd place each guy; I'd place all the guys—maybe five—along the road. Then maybe two of us would go in or I'd go alone. I'd head back into that bush, I'd run that hardwood ridge, or the side of it; sometimes I'd spot two or three deer. Just going. Ahhh! They're heading for the guys up there.

You know, those guys were never where I put them.

They'd move, or they'd be sitting there with a fire going and the guns all leaning up against a tree. They'd be smoking and the deer would come right out across the road there, across a whole big space where the river was flowing. And there's lots of time to knock them off, and there the hunters are—they've built a fire, or two of them are visiting, having their smokes, and they've put their rifles down somewhere. Deer go *zzzoom*—right on by! And sometimes maybe the deer don't go by; maybe they stop right on the edge of that road and stand there for a long time and watch. They see those guys. They just know when. All of a sudden they walk out onto the road and the guy looks at them; he goes to get his rifle—*tchk, tchk, tchk*—they're gone! But they'll walk out on the road. If he just had a rifle in his hand he'd just have to raise it —POW!—and there would be his deer. But never like that.

And when you get close to them you start hollering, "Hoo, hay-a, hay there!" And then you break branches and you whistle, "Hoo, hay, hoo." That's what you do, because you've got to do that or they might shoot you. So you make one drive in there. Then you take them down further and you place them again. And that is guiding.

I just don't know why they go hunting, those guys. I really don't know, except they seem to doubt their manhood and want to prove themselves. But I don't know what that has to do with manhood: a little frail deer and a guy with a gun that could kill an elephant. But they're hung up somehow on that manhood thing. The truth is most of them are scared shitless of the bush. And it's strange how they just don't learn. I've had guys three years in a row, and they even seem to be dumber in that third year than they've ever been and they still don't know anything. I don't know what happens to them, what they experience. Nothing! I would have to be right with each guy, see, baby-sitting. They're experiencing it but it doesn't seem to mean a damn thing. I came along once and here's a guy with wet feet. He'd been sliding on the ice in the creek and broke through. And he was stamping his feet and shivering, other guys standing around. And I said, "Hey, what happened to you just now?" Almost as if I had to get hold of him and shake him up, let him see what was going on. "Jesus, your feet got wet and it's pretty cold, eh?" Then I got a fire going, told him to get his boots off, dry his feet. A large part of guiding is just goddam baby-sitting.

I was well liked at that camp. The woman who owned the place used to say, "Wilfred, what the hell are you doing here?" I don't know what was in her mind when she asked me that—maybe it was that I was literate and worked and lived in town in the same way whites do. But I was a guide. I don't know what her idea of a guide was, because all the hunters who had me as their guide wanted me back the next year. To her that seemed to mean I was too good for a guide. Crazy, eh? One thing was that they could communicate with me—what they call communication. Most Indian guides wouldn't talk; they wouldn't tell the hunters anything. They'd just take them out. But I'd already been exposed for a little while to that white world, and I also knew about hunting and all that even though I wasn't an old hand at guiding. I only guided maybe three or four years all together, so I never was very experienced as a guide. But I explained things to the hunters, and I talked to them. I sometimes worked with other guides and they would just look down at the ground reading the signs; look around and figure out just where the deer might be. Then they would go there and never bother explaining anything.

I guess most hunters sort of look down on the guide. He's paid help, after all, a kind of servant. But few hunters have any idea of how the guide sees them. Most of those old men didn't talk because they couldn't see any point in trying to explain something to a guy who carried a roll of store string in his pocket so he wouldn't get lost. What would you say to anyone that ignorant, that helpless? But I talked to them and explained what I was doing, and maybe that made a difference. Anyway, a lot of them would get back to camp and say, "That Wilfred's a great guide. Boy, he's a good guide!" But I wasn't really; I couldn't touch any of those other guides there. Those old men were out of sight! Nobody had any idea how good they were. They could survive anywhere. Strong. Tough. And some of them were over seventy.

See, it wasn't the good guide, it was Wilf Pelletier—a good Joe. But I was strict; I learned to be very strict from the old men. They told me one of the worst things that could happen to a guide was to lose a man or have a man die on you, have a guy get lost or have somebody shot in your group. If that ever happens, you'll lose face not only as a guide but as an Indian. And that's important, boy. I would tell those hunters, "I don't care whether you wash your hands before you cook fish or before you clean out a deer. That isn't important; you're going to come out alive. If you go in with me, I'm going to bring you back out, or I'm going to die trying." And to me that was a law; I had all that written into me, as an individual, from the old men. So it didn't matter how the hunters saw me because I knew they couldn't make a move without me. I was king where I was; I knew that. And that whole concept they had about Indians—well, I could ignore that, anyway.

Part of that was they were usually uptight about giving me booze because I was Indian. That never bothered me a great deal. For one thing, I didn't drink very much. Well, I didn't mind an occasional drink and sometimes . . . yes, I'd get loaded. When that happened, I was usually with a bunch of friends. It was a whole fun thing. I'd had lots of experience before of that whole Indian putdown thing, so I always recognized it when it came along: Well, okay, here it is again. And I didn't get hostile, I didn't tell anybody off, I did it in a nice way; tried to tell them I wasn't any different than them except that when I drank I was pretty free, see, and I knew that they were hung up on behavior. So I never drank with any of them very much. I'd go over there and they'd want to talk; they'd want to take up all my time talking about the woods and experiences in the bush. And then they'd really try to do it in a nice way—turning me down for drinks. Well, you know, when you come in from hunting and it's cold and you're with a guy half the day, maybe, while the other guys are strung out all over, you get to kind of know him. Then he says to come on over to the cabin for a drink, so you go there in all good faith. But pretty soon you see a couple together and they're talking and you don't know what they're saying, but you suspect it's "Jesus, we shouldn't give the guide anything to drink." So nothing is said, but everyone is drinking and no one offers you a drink.

Of course, I knew that was the policy of a lot of tourist-camp operators: "Don't give our Indian guides anything to drink. They don't know when to stop and they'll drink all night"—stuff like that. I knew that, so I didn't drink much because I wasn't going to have anyone push me around.

So there's a whole thing about Indians and liquor, another piece of the popular mythology that's very old. Many people still think that the way Indians react to alcohol is due to some physical difference, that they have a different chemistry. And that's a very bad misconception because if you believe that, it's almost as if Indians are not quite human. They forget that Indians have a whole different view of life—a different life-style—and the way Indians react to liquor is probably appropriate to that life-style. In most cases, anyway.

There are other factors, too, that sometimes make alcohol a special problem for Indian people. There are still some reserves where drinking is against the law, so Indians go into town and buy a bottle or maybe two. They can't take it home and drink it, and it's against the law to drink in a public place. So what do they do? They go in a back alley or maybe in a men's can and they knock the whole bottle off real quick. So then there are some drunken Indians staggering around the town, because drinking that fast will knock anybody on his ass.

Personally, I don't think booze is all that great, for whites or Indians. It's a white-man thing. It fits his culture; otherwise it wouldn't be legal. It's what makes it possible for millions of people to put up with being regimented, to go through that whole putdown routine of earning a living day after day doing something that doesn't call for the ability or talent of an imbecile. There has to be some explanation.

Anyway, I had that whole booze thing to put up with. And so did the hunters, because most of them really wanted to be hospitable and friendly. So they'd come along to me, and they just sort of tried to put it in the best way they could. Most of them wouldn't offer me any drink at all because I'm Indian—like, I go wild when I drink! So they wouldn't offer me the drink. But then sometimes a guy would. He'd ask me, though; he'd say, "This stuff won't get to you, will it, chief?" And I'd say, "Well, I don't know. Don't you ever get drunk?" And he'd say, "Oh, yeah." "Well, I get drunk too, sometimes," I'd say. And sometimes if it was done in a way that I didn't feel too bad, and yet I knew he was feeling bad, I'd tell him, "Well, you know what you're talking about is behavior. You have to behave a certain way when you drink; I don't. And that's the difference between you and me. I can just be myself and if I want to holler I'll holler, but you don't dare holler because too many people are going to make judgments about your behavior." So I said, "If I have a good time, I have a damned good time when I get drunk and that's all I do. But you have moral hang-ups about it, see, which is pretty silly." If I felt that I wanted to I'd talk like that, but most of the time it was no use. They believed I was just a dirty Indian and didn't know nothing. If I wanted a drink I would bring my own bottle. And I did, but I drank with the old men and some of the guys I worked with. We'd have a couple of drinks and go to bed. Play cards or something. And we'd tell stories and talk. Never planned the next day. Never. Well, maybe I'd say, "I'm going down by Garden Lake tomorrow," and they'd say, "I think I'll take my group back down by the dam." That's about all.

The guides and the hunters—what a contrast! If the guides could tell the hunters what being in that bush means to them—now, that would be worth something. To the guide that bush is home and he is kin to everything that lives there. But to the hunters it was getting away, it was a big drunk, it was sport, it was buying deer or buying moose or bear . . . and it didn't matter so long as they went home with a trophy. And some of them went home with this or that carcass, but some of them, of course, went home without it. Sometimes out of a group of six, four would get a deer. But it wasn't only game they took home. They also took home stories, and I would never know how the stories might change after they left. I remember two guys in the group one year and they took home a deer. The feedback I got was that those guys both fired at the same time, so it belonged to both of them. They didn't know which one got it. The truth is that I shot the deer for them and gave it to them. And they took it home and they said, "Well, this belongs to both Phil and me because we both shot at it and one of us hit it but we don't know which one." Those stories would come back to me and I would have a good laugh.

But I became aware that behind all that talk there was something pretty desperate. Those guys all came there together and they were supposed to be good friends and all that. But they weren't buddies, they were rivals. Out of a party of four or five, one would get a deer, then another and another, till maybe there was only one guy or maybe two who hadn't shot a deer. And the guys who had shot deer would be strutting around, just couldn't help it. And they'd start teasing the other guy, putting him down. But underneath all that kidding they were telling him, "Hey, take a look at a man." I've even heard them say that when they'd come in with a deer: "I'm a man." Somehow, getting a deer made them a man. And I noticed they probably got drunk that night and used more profanity than usual because all that had something to do with manhood too. Well, I'm the guide. I'd sit there listening and watching all this going on, and after a while I'd get kind of sick to my stomach and I'd have to leave.

But there was a fascination, too, in listening to those guys. Otherwise I don't think I would have ever gone near them except strictly as a guide. Never socially. I think it must have been the lies that attracted me; I just couldn't believe them. They'd tell stories while just sitting around at night. The evenings would consist of heavy boozing usually, card playing perhaps, and remembering last year's hunt. Last year's two weeks off they had at the plant. Well, the plant would be included in almost everything. Or "down at the shop," or "the office": all the businesses would be brought in during the evening. And they'd talk about their business and about how some guy, "Fred, you know, he used to be a hunter . . . well, I deal with Fred, I manufacture reams, you know"—whatever those are—and of course Fred's company buys them. And then there would be a big buildup about all the money they got, and all that kind of stuff. This is all for me, see. They're letting me know I'm the stranger. These guys all know each other, so they don't have to go into all that, but they do for me. But they don't talk to me, they talk to each other. It's crazy.

Impressing the Indian! So I'd sit there and I'd listen to all that. Then they'd get to talking about last year's hunt. And I was *there* last year! I guided them, or at least some of these guys, and the stories have become monstrous now. They're big. Like, "That deer that Shack got over there, that was a long haul. That must have been three miles to haul that deer out of those woods. Boy, remember that? That was really tough." Well, it was Wilf Pelletier who dragged that damned deer out for Shack last year.

And I'm listening to all this. But there's one or two new guys each year that come with the old group; maybe some guy'll drop off and there's another instead. So there's always these big stories going on for the benefit of the new guy. Then they'd talk about hunting coons, and I got to listen about hunting coons in Ohio or somewhere down in their country. Then they'd talk of pigs because some of those guys were farmers—pig farmers.

Those pig farmers! I never would have believed you could talk about pigs for hours on end, but they could—and they did. All about what they fed them and the best breeds and the best crosses and how much the government was paying them for *not* growing certain crops. And pig diseases and the best way to treat those—there was no end to it. They even had their pigs named. A guy would say, "Do you remember old Sarah? Best old sow I ever did see. Why, she'd have eighteen, twenty piglets every litter. I never knew her to have less than sixteen. And I never knew her to roll on one or step on one. Gentle as a kitten she was." And he'd sit there, kind of shaking his head and looking at the floor, thinking about Sarah. Then he'd say, "You know, when she died I just broke down and cried. Cried like a baby. I ain't ashamed to admit it. She was just like one of the family. The wife, she cried too. I got that sow from Jim Beam over in Greene County. You know Jim Beam." Then they'd get into a long conversation about Jim Beam and *his* pigs.

That same bunch from Ohio came back every year. And every year I'd hear those same stories all over again. Well, the last year I went guiding we were sitting around one night and one of them asked me, "Wilf, what do you do when you're not guiding? I guess you just sit around and live good on all the money you make off us guys." And they all laughed because that was supposed to be a joke, you see—*and* a sort of dig, because all those farmers were tight-assed as hell and thought the price of guides was pretty heavy. Well, I don't know what came over me; it must have been that I was sick of hearing all those pig stories. Anyway, I said, "Oh, I'd never attempt to live on the money I get from guiding. Matter of fact, I only go guiding for the hell of it. I enjoy being out in the bush, and fall and winter are sort of the off season for me anyway. But I don't need the money. I've got a good business of my own." When I said that, they really sat up and took notice because here was an ignorant Indian talking about being in business. Then the same guy asked me, "What business are you in?" and I knew I had him. So I took a big breath and keeping a very straight face, I said, "The eel business." "The eel business?" he says, looking very surprised. "Yup," I went on, "I've got a really big eel ranch up one of the rivers that runs into Lake Nipigon." "Well, I never!" he says. "I wouldn't have thought there was all that much call for eels." "Oh yes," I assured him, "eels are considered a great delicacy in many places. Especially England. We shipped over eight tons last year to England alone. Some frozen, some in cans." "Is that a fact?" he says. "There must be a hell of a lot of them. But I'd think at that rate you'll have them all fished out pretty quick." "Oh, no," I told him, "that's the great thing about eels; you just can't fish them out. No way. Some salt-water fish, like salmon and shad, come up the rivers to spawn. Eels are just the opposite: they go down the rivers to spawn. Down to the sea. Every fall, they leave. Every spring, back they come. And they bring all their babies with them." "Well I'll be damned," he says. "And about how many eggs will an eel lay?" "Depends on the size of the eel," I

[95]

told him. "An average-size eel will probably lay maybe ten million. I've got one old sow eel—Georgia, I call her. She's a whopper—about seven feet long and she must go over eighty pounds. I expect she lays upwards of fifty million." "Wow!" he says.

"Of course," I hurried to explain, "she doesn't bring fifty million babies back with her. The mortality rate is something fierce. Most of them get eaten by fish and so on. Over ninety-nine percent never make it. But even so, I guess she gets back to the river with over a hundred thousand babies—most years, anyway. And they're very small, you know, only a couple of inches long. Time they make that long journey with her to the sea and back, for six more years, which is when we begin to harvest them, there's a lot more casualities. So out of fifty million eggs, we end up with maybe ten thousand eels. Maybe less. But of course, Georgia's not the only sow. There's lots more. All smaller than her."

"Well!" he says, "you learn something new every day. But I guess in different parts of the world, people will eat just about any damn thing. I once heard of a tribe in Africa eats caterpillars. Can you imagine?"

I did have a regular job, but I used to get time off to go guiding. And I don't know why I did that except it was a way I could be with my own people, especially the old men, and speak my own language. The other part is that I was lazy and always looking for a way to get out of work. Actually, guiding is very hard work, but I was young and strong and it seemed like fun.

It sounds crazy, but I knew part of it was that all my

life I was motivated to get out of work. There was something in my nature that objected to work. I've always called it laziness, but maybe that isn't the right name for it. I can remember running away when I was a kid at home because my father wanted me to pile a cord of wood. Running away, and being gone for three days, and eating seagulls' eggs and a few berries and getting really hungry and sleeping out in the bush. All that just to get out of piling a cord of wood. I guess I really don't understand yet what all that's about. And you see, one of the types that I became very much aware of in Sault Sainte Marie— there were a lot of them around—was white guys who were a little on the fat side, always smoking a cigar; they talked with a lot of authority, never seemed to do anything very much, but they seemed to be into a lot of things. And I regarded them as successful people. I never dreamed they were mortgaged to the hilt and probably didn't have a penny. All I could see was that they had other people working for them. So, when I started getting into a business of my own, I was thinking, you know, I'll have to work pretty hard to get this thing going and so on but pretty soon I won't have to do that. I'll hire a manager and then I can sit back. I didn't admire those guys but I envied them their apparent wealth and apparent ease. I didn't see at the time that it was a whole game they were playing, that it was all just a front, and that they really weren't very successful people. Most of them were barely managing to keep themselves afloat, I expect, and putting most of their energy into keeping up that front.

One of the first things I discovered about mainstream society was that everyone seemed to be into something called work. They even took pride in it. But to me, being lazy, it seemed more like a disease. For a while I thought playing baseball would get me out of the work thing; I was just going to play and get paid for playing. But I was mistaken about that. When you *have* to play, then play becomes work.

After making that discovery I looked around for an easier way to survive and got a job at a laundry driving a truck, picking up and delivering. It was great. I got to know most of the people in the town, some of them in a pretty intimate way. Well, I worked my way up through that pretty fast and became manager of a dry-cleaning plant. And of course I dressed the part: white shirt and tie and a suit, nice shiny shoes—polished my shoes all the time. I even wore white socks at one time. Oh yeah! And then I had to get a coat with a label on it because everybody had coats with some kind of crest. So I bought one and I had a crest sewn onto it. I don't remember what crest it was, it just had Moosonee or something written on it, but there was a crest! Theirs all had crowns and anchors, but I wasn't related to anything with the crown or the navy. I'm here and I've always been here. So that's how I got launched into that whole damn business: attempting to become somebody.

Can you imagine? Becoming! Attempting to become . . . somebody. Becoming a success. I guess that drive to become successful is regarded as a virtue and is called ambition. That must be in ratio to your opinion of yourself: the more unacceptable you find yourself, the more you are driven to become somebody. That must be what ambition is. If that is true, I must have had a very low opinion of myself back in those days because in the next three years I became the owner-manager of a restaurant where I worked twelve hours a day doing the cooking. That was a full-time job. Then I became the owner of a ladies' apparel shop that my wife Dorrie ran. Then I became a partner in a construction outfit that put up prefabricated houses. And then I had a grocery store a hundred-odd miles out of town where I drove out and back twice a week; took stock, worked there for several hours each time. I really wanted to become successful! It was the same as the school trip, only I guess I'd got a lot dumber than when I was a kid, because I didn't get hooked on the school trip but I was hooked on this one. I didn't even see the connection till years later. School was for kids: that's why you didn't take it seriously. But this was business; this was for men. I guess that's where my head was at.

For the next five years I was in that restaurant and all those other businesses. The restaurant became the Elpelco Restaurant Company Limited. I owned something called Norgom Real Estate. I was a successful businessman drawing a small wage. I was still as lazy as ever, but I was working long hours and I was very tired. I was on my feet so long every day that my feet would bleed. Lots of times when I finally got home at night, it would take half an hour to soak the socks off my feet. But I was still going at it because I hadn't made any money.

No money. But credit—did I have credit! Everybody was wanting to give me things. Guys would come down and let me drive their car for a week: "Here—try this car out." They'd want me to buy a car. And somebody else next week would bring me another car. So I had a car for quite a while, from different companies in town, and never owned any of them. I thought I was really a big shot. But every few days there'd be something in my life that would happen, and it kept telling me, "Wilfred, that's not who you are. What are you doing, anyhow? What is

this merry-go-round you're on? That's not who you are!"
Not only would something tell me, I'd feel all that thing
out. Then sometimes I'd run into somebody. Suddenly,
here's another Indian person and he's drunk as hell. So I'd
take him home and put him to bed. And sometimes I
would know him, but more often I wouldn't. And I can
remember standing, looking at those guys sleeping there
on the nice clean sheets. Some of them were dirty, sure—
whatever that means to you—and sometimes they smelled
of puke. And I knew all about the white loathing of that
sort of thing. But I didn't feel that way. I wasn't able to
make any judgment. I was glad I had found the guy and
got him home before the police got him. But I had mixed
feelings because I was an Indian trying to make it in the
white man's world.

Next morning I'd be gone before the guy woke up.
Later on, Dorrie would tell me about the guy waking up,
not knowing where he was or how he got there—how he
ate a big breakfast while she learned he was from Cutler
or Garden River or someplace. And it usually turned out
he was somebody's uncle or grandfather, someone we
knew.

I identified with those people. Drunk or sober, dirty or
clean, they were my people. Still, there was conflict in me,
a confusion. I expect all urban Indians experience it. It's
losing your people. You see, all that time I was growing
up I didn't know I was Indian. It was when I moved into
Western society that I found that out. I also found out that
I was lazy, shiftless, illiterate, no good, drunk, even savage
and non-Christian. Well, I didn't like being any of those
things—because I wasn't, except maybe lazy. But I knew
I had no choice; I had to put up with all those categories
because they were all firmly embedded in white people's
minds. I didn't realize that wasn't my problem. I didn't

know at the time that it was really the problem of all those whites. Only later I discovered that was all theirs. Somebody had done that to them. And I felt sorry for them. But at the time, I was just looking for any way at all to escape from all that Indian putdown. So I thought, Well if I put another L in my name and an E, it will sound French. And that's what I'll become: French. And Indian, if it becomes necessary for me to admit it. And sometimes people would ask me, they'd say, "Oh, French, eh?" And I wouldn't even answer them—just let them think I'm French. But some of those persistent bastards would say, "But you're not just French." Then I'd say, "No, I'm part Indian," or if I was mad I'd say, "I'm Indian." I suppose all that may have helped me to get by, but I didn't feel very good about it.

There were no recognized Indian organizations at that time. Indians were the hidden people. Even though Indians came into town and bought things in the stores and so on, the white community tended to ignore the Indian people and were really, I think, embarrassed by the presence of Indians. And I was into that too. I had the experience of being in some kind of store talking to the proprietor. Just visiting a fellow businessman. And we'd both be all dressed up in our business uniforms—white shirt, tie, suit. Then some Indians would come into the store. The men would have on big boots, all muddy, pants rolled up, an old shirt, maybe a guide license pinned on it somewhere. The women would be wearing cheap cotton dresses and sweaters, kerchiefs tied over their hair, cotton stockings, and sneakers. And they would talk in monosyllables and point at what they wanted. The silent presence of those people—my people—was an embarrassment to me. That's what bad shape I was in.

I was split or torn, trying to be two people. But even

though it nearly killed me, that double life, I continued to hang around with Indians. I used to go down quite often to Garden River, which was the closest reserve to Sault Sainte Marie. I hunted down there all the time on the reserve. I had a lot of friends there. Before I was married I went with Indian girls on the Garden River Reserve. So I maintained that relationship, and of course, every chance I got I went home, I went back down to Wikwemikong.

One thing I never did in my attempt to become somebody was disregard my people, because I kept going back there. But because of that stereotype, all those things about Indians, I never knew how people saw me. People knew I was Indian or got to know that, and I didn't know whether they were learning that here's Wilf Pelletier, see, and before there were just Indians. Because Indians were all categorized as the same. But they knew me personally and I wasn't drunk and I wasn't no-good, none of those putdown things that all Indians are supposed to be. So that whole thing I went through, really struggling for whatever was inside of me, you see, kept telling me . . . I don't know . . . I don't think it would have been possible for me ever to make a decision that would have taken me completely out of being Indian, out of my true identity. I guess I was alternating between slavery and freedom, not just in what I was doing, but also in the sense of who I was.

Every chance I got, no matter how tired I was, I went fishing. Then I felt free. I felt something about who I was, even though I thought I was only playing a role when I went fishing. Since I couldn't survive as an Indian *and* a businessman, I'd go and *play* Indian. I thought I was really a businessman, but it was the reverse. I talked In-

dian all the time, so I was really being me. The *rest* was
a game, the restaurant, the whole business thing was the
game, but at the time I didn't know it. I thought, Well, I'll
just play Indian because eventually all that will go. Business is what I'm supposed to be doing. That is where it's
at: making it in the business world; becoming somebody.

So we'd go fishing, Dolph and I, in the bush all the
time. And hunting in the fall, with partridge all over and
lots of ducks. Later in the fall, it was deer and moose.
Those are things I never missed. But that fishing! Every
week, two or three times a week, after work those long
summer days, I'd carry a canoe a couple of miles in, over
hills, through the bush. Maybe I'd carry it in and Dolph
would carry it out. And we talked only Indian, all the
time. Sometimes we'd never get to the lake. We'd run into
a bees' nest and then we'd have fun. Or we'd run into a
bear, spot a bear coming up the trail, ambling along. So
we'd put the canoe aside, and then we'd sit there very still
and wait until that bear came right up close to us hiding
behind the trees, and then we'd jump out—the two of us
—"YAHHHHHH!!!" That damned bear would take off
and he'd go right through brush piles, trees, deadfalls;
he'd hit them and they'd just break and go way up in the
air! And we'd lie on the ground and laugh and laugh—I'm
telling you, our sides would be sore, we'd be holding
ourselves, we couldn't get up or we'd piss in our pants or
something! Dolph wore glasses, and what a time! The first
time he lost his glasses and we hunted and hunted, I bet
you three hours. Well, it got dark on us before we found
them. Just happened to step on the corner and they
popped up in the leaves—he'd never have found them
otherwise. So we never got fishing that time, just went
back home. But after that he'd put his glasses up some-

where, so we'd know where they were. And all that fun, that playing around, that freedom, all that was the real me. If those people back in Sault Ste. Marie could have seen me! What a businessman! They would never have recognized me.

That's funny, isn't it? What is a businessman? There's this thing in mainstream society about growing up, becoming serious about things. I guess "acting your age" is restraining yourself, inhibiting yourself. And that's pretty old too. It's even in the Bible—"When I became a man I put away childish things." Maybe that's where all that bullshit started. Indians don't grow up that way. They get wiser and, I guess, more responsible, but they never forget the fun of childhood. And the kids don't exclude adults. They'll be playing hockey on the road with a frozen horse bun for a puck and some old guy will come along. They'll give him a stick: "Come on, Grandpa, take a shot, show us how!" I never have been able to understand why fun seems to be prohibited in white society. But we had fun.

We really studied the fishing, too. I knew when they were biting and what depth they were biting at and what to use. Depending on what lake it was, we knew just how to fish it, so we'd always come home with fish. We'd be loaded with fish when we came back from out there. Talk about fish galore! Then somebody'd find the lake and two years later there'd be no fish in there; they'd fished it all out. So we'd have to find another lake. We kept doing that. Fishing . . . we never took it seriously, always put back the small ones. Even the big ones we'd put back. At first we used to take them, but later on we put them all back in the water no matter what size. Sometimes we'd injure some, so we'd bring them home. But we'd often catch three or four times more than we could ever take home.

It got to be that the fun out of that whole thing was just being in the bush, and little things, crazy things, like kicking through leaves, sitting on a log beside a little stream, maybe getting a drink of cold water, lying down and getting a nice drink. And then sitting on a log, and maybe Dolph would have a smoke—I didn't smoke much then. We'd sit there, talking in Indian, just about the bush, mostly, about our experiences or how we felt about something. No hurry about anything. And maybe he'd pick something, a stone or a fungus; he'd always be picking up little things. Both of us would, but especially Dolph. He'd spot things all over and he'd bring them over and we'd look at them and talk about them. I think that kept me sane through those crazy years. Talking my own language: that was like music to me. And being in the bush.

And the other thing—going to Garden River Reserve all the time; that's where I did a lot of fishing and hunting. I spoke Indian with Dolph, but there were very few people on that reserve who spoke Indian—mostly the older people—so I'd seek them out so I could speak my own language. And then there'd be people who'd come from our reserve, passing through, and they'd stop at our place. They'd usually stay overnight. Then I'd get a chance again to talk in my own language. And that kept me speaking it all the time, reminding me of who I was. Then I'd feel really good, good enough to go back on the old business trip again.

Finally, going in the bush all the time, I began to realize people weren't seeing me any more. And that's what I thought I wanted, you know. I was Indian and it wasn't very good to be Indian; Indians weren't "in." So people weren't seeing me any more, but I was being affected by that: I wasn't seeing me any more either. That's what scared me. That whole identity thing is pretty interesting, how you actually create it and build it and build it. I guess it was pretty hard for most people in that part of the country in those days to imagine there could be such a thing as a successful Indian. Maybe their way of handling that was just to see me as one of them. And of course, that had to be white. After a while, they just didn't see the Indian any more.

I was Wilf Pelletier, and you know, if you don't mention the Indian, why, that's okay. At first it was Wilf Pelletier. Then after a while it got to be Mr. Pelletier, and then there got to be the Elpelco Restaurant and all those other businesses. So pretty soon it's "Yes sir!" and "No sir!" and "What can I do for you, sir?" Then the credit thing, a sure sign of success. I was approached by the Junior Chamber of Commerce to join their organization and I was supposed to go to church, I suppose because it looked good for the business community if I went to church. I didn't really join the Junior Chamber of Commerce, but I went two or three times. And the first thing I ran into was some kind of thing called the "Toastmaster's Club." Anyway, it's a public-speaking thing. They get you to speak, because every young businessman is supposed to be able to get up, impromptu, and make a speech and supposed to know all about parliamentary procedure and how to chair a meeting and all that. Well, that was it for me. I couldn't think of a word to say. And you know, they even had a proper lingo, a sort of business-man's jargon: this is the proper way to say this and to say that. I wasn't used to that and I guess it was—to me it was awfully phony. I was used to saying "Hi, George!" or "What do you know, Tommy?" or "Hey, Jim, come on over here and take a look at this." But now I was being told that I was supposed to say, "Hello, Mr. Johnston.

Would you kindly step this way, please? I would like to show you something." It seemed to me that all that was alienating. It would alienate you from other people, alienate you from reality, and get you into a whole phony performance.

I also joined the Rod and Gun Club, and that was a strange experience. Dolph and I both joined. We were the only Indians in it, and that's why I say it was strange. Both of us had hunted and fished all our lives, but to us that had never been a recreation, and we had never thought of it as sport. It wasn't something you did on weekends or even in hunting season; it was just part of a way of life. Something you enjoyed, sure, but it wasn't special. I guess that's what I mean.

In a way, being in that club was a whole replay of my guiding experience. Most of the guys in the club were the same kind of people I had met as a guide—big bullshitters. Dolph and I used to talk about that because we were the silent members, and I remember asking him if he thought they really believed all those stories they told each other. He said no, he didn't think any bullshitter ever believed another because they all knew how one fish became a dozen and how ten ounces got to be ten pounds. But you didn't question another guy's story: that was an unwritten rule.

There was another thing in that club that, to me, was really weird: secrecy. The whole club was broken up into little cliques and each one was into a big act about where they hunted or where they fished. All very mysterious; they had found some really great hunting or fishing but they weren't telling anyone where it was. The crazy thing was that Dolph and I got more fish and deer than anyone and we told everyone where we went.

It's maybe ten years since I shot a deer. That's because
I now live in a big urban area and deer hunting is not part
of that scene. I get my meat at the supermarket. I may
never hunt deer again, but if I do, I won't be going on any
big expedition; I'll just be going out to shoot a deer because I need something to eat and I like deer meat. And
I won't put on any special outfit to do that. I'll wear
something warm and comfortable and boots that will keep
my feet dry. I don't have any place in my closet where all
that is hanging up, you see—my hunting outfit. And I
don't have any cabinet on the wall with all my guns in
there. A sort of display case of masculinity, I guess. Hell,
I don't even have a gun!

Anyway, that's how it will be. I won't even be looking
for deer to start with. I'll just be looking the country over,
enjoying the luxury of being out there, looking it all over,
casually, like turning the pages of a picture book. And I'll
see mouse tracks and squirrel tracks and rabbit tracks and
partridge tracks and droppings of all sorts. Then I'll see
some deer tracks—fresh too, maybe. Then . . . ah, they've
been feeding here. And they went that way . . . That's how
I'll get my deer: by reading the signs and knowing from
those signs where the deer are most likely to be, not by
driving around the back roads in a pickup truck hoping
I'll get a shot at something. I don't know what you'd call
that, but it's not hunting. And it can be dangerous.

A lot of people object to hunting. And so do I, but in
a different way—not because of taking a life or anything
like that. I have never been able to see it as a sport; I just
don't understand that. It's fun; exciting but serious too, as
serious as religion. Taking a life is a religious act, or
should be. And this competitive thing—who bags the biggest deer or lands the heaviest fish—that turns my stom-

ach. Hunting is part of a total way of life, just as maple sugaring is. And you have the same reverence for those animals as you have for those trees that sustain you. In an Indian community the best hunters hunt for the whole community. Just so with the best fishermen. But that doesn't make those hunters and fishermen any better or any more manly than anyone else.

When I was a boy, one of the great hunters and fishers in our community was Che-Dominic. Che-Dominic had a big family to feed—ten or twelve kids—but even so, when people knew he'd been hunting they'd show up at his place. Sure enough, there'd be a deer or maybe two or three hanging in the yard. When Che-Dominic saw them admiring his kill, he'd invite them to help with the skinning, then, *"Dopenon whayamun,"* he'd say. "Help yourself."

Che-Dominic never went hunting; He went out to shoot a deer. He knew exactly when and where to go, and when, as rarely happened, he wasn't successful, he'd say, with a thoughtful look, *"Gego edik gosicheganong"* (I must have done something I shouldn't have done). And I knew he'd go back over his whole day in his mind, to find out what that thing was.

I liked Che-Dominic, liked just being with him, and whenever I could I would go out with him for deer. He would just start out walking, me following. At some point, maybe quite close by or other times after we had walked a long way, he'd stop and sit down. Then he would say, "We'll just wait here. He'll come to us." I still don't know how he knew that. It was as if he called them. He would say, *"Kun do kun,"* and I guess that is deer talk because I really cannot explain what it means. It has the feeling of drawing the deer to you, calling them. But that was only part of it. The other part was that the deer knew he was there and needed food, but it didn't seem to me that they were coming to be slaughtered. It was like they were coming near enough to give us a chance to kill them if we were alert and skillful enough to do that, but no more than a chance.

◻════◻════◻

I suppose being in that club helped me in business. Most of those people respected me and liked me. After five years I was pretty well accepted in that town—as a businessman, not as an Indian. The Indian part was just overlooked. But I didn't give a damn about being accepted. What I really wanted was success—money, and the freedom that money can bring. And after five years I still didn't have any money. The whole situation was getting tighter and tighter. I had less and less time I could take off to go fishing. And when Dolph and I did go, we were now like white people: rushing off to get in two or three hours of fishing and then back to work again. But sometimes when I was out there fishing I would have moments of sanity. And I would think, What the hell am I doing with all this busyness? What am I doing?

Finally I began to develop tension headaches, really bad headaches. When I went to the doctor, he said that I had to take three weeks off. Three weeks off! I could hardly believe it! So I loaded up my car with fishing gear and took off, alone.

Free! What a beautiful feeling. My first vacation in over five years. I was tired, but excited too. The car was speeding north to where the fish were waiting, blue sky of early spring . . . flowers . . . and bushes, trees, rocks flying—darkness . . .

It is morning, and the sun is warm for April. I am
walking on the beach to the little creek that comes in at
the head of the Bay. I can see it coming closer. The willows along its banks are blood-red with sap. Then I am
there. The creek is swollen and a little muddy. The banks
near its mouth are undercut and grassy, but the grass is
dead and pressed flat from the winter's snow. The creek
is full of suckers, come to spawn.

I roll up my sleeve, high as I can, and lie down on the
bank. I put my arm down into the icy water and reaching
in under the bank, feel around very slowly. Oops! Too
clumsy. The fish is scared off. I move a few feet along the
bank and try again. Ah, there he is. Now, very, very
gently underneath, along his belly up toward his gills and
. . . now! I've got him. Throw him well up the bank. A big
one.

All day, up and down the banks, working both sides of
the creek, I tickle suckers. At noon, I eat my lunch and
think about the kids in school. Then, back at it. Along
about four, four thirty in the afternoon I have so many
fish I am just amazed. I don't know what to do with all of
them. I think, Well, I'll take home what I can and I'll hide
the rest under some old dead leaves here. So that's what
I do. I'll come back and get those ones I've hidden on the
second trip. Then I go over to where the willows are
growing and cut a long willow stick with a crotch at the
bottom of it, and I string all those fish on that stick, all
kinds of fish. Then I bring the two ends around together
so I can get ahold of them. But I have so many fish I can't
lift them, so I drag them along the sand. I am just starting
to drag those fish home when a boy comes out and just
stands there. He lives in a house close by—it's the only
house around there. And I know he's come to get my fish.

He's a little bigger than I am; I think he is at least a year, maybe two years older. Well, nobody is going to get those fish away from me, that's for sure. I'm going to fight. But I'm impressed by this kid. He's pretty husky and I guess I'm afraid of him. But nobody is going to get those fish.

So he stands there. Then he speaks to me in Indian: "*Ani.*" (Hello.)

And I say, "*Ani.*"

"*Ambesh ayshyian?*" (Where are you going?)

"*Andouang.*" (Home.)

I keep walking, dragging my fish, taking a few steps between each question and answer. And he keeps moving up, getting nearer and nearer.

"Where do you live?" he asks.

"Wikwemikong."

"What's your name?"

"Wilfred."

We are getting closer and closer and I'm getting pretty scared. Then he says, "You know, I could pound the shit out of you."

I don't say anything; just keep dragging my fish along. Then he is standing right in front of me, blocking my way: "Do you want me to beat you up?"

I try to get around him, first one side then the other, still dragging the fish. Then he says, "*Neen dibenmok gee-gon.*" (I own those fish.)

All of a sudden I drop the fish, wheel around, and kick that guy. I knock him down, I jump on him, I kick him some more. I'm right out of my head. I have bare feet; my shoes are tied together and strung over my shoulder because they're soaking wet. Well, I fight that guy and in spite of all I've done to him he still gets up and pounds the hell out of me. But I have an advantage: I've really hurt him to begin with. So I really fight back. I think I took half the fight out of him right off the bat. Finally I pick up my fish again and start dragging them down the beach. We're both crying; he's crying, I'm crying. He's lying there on the beach, and as I pull those fish away he gets up and stands there. I can see him standing back there, watching me go. Then when I am a long ways away from him and I think I'm home free, he picks up a stick that is lying off to one side and takes after me. And I pull those fish and I pull them and I can't run and he is getting closer and closer and that is a pretty big stick. I wait till he gets right up to me—then I drop the fish and start to run. Well, he can't catch me. Maybe it's because he has that stick to carry and can't run as well. Anyway, I'm really running and dodging from side to side and going up that beach to beat hell. I get away, but I lose my fish.

My enemy gave up the chase and turned back. But I ran all the way home, not because I was afraid; there was nothing now to be afraid of, but because I *had* to run. I was filled, totally overwhelmed, with feelings of helplessness, rage and frustration. It was like a huge, black cloud hanging over me. I ran to get out from under that cloud . . .

◻◼◼◼◻◼◼◼◻

I came to with a flashlight shining in my eyes. The cops drove me in to emergency at Little Current. I was lucky—only some broken ribs—but the car was a total wreck. My chest was really sore, but I only stayed in bed two days. Then I got Dorrie to come down and pick me up, and away I went again. All I could think of, even with all that pain, was I'm off for three weeks! I got my cousin Alphonse to go with me, hired a plane, and took off up north. Within a few days I was packing a canoe around on my back and to hell with the broken ribs. We had some great fishing. It was one of the best times I ever had in my life. Except for one thing.

All the time we were away I kept thinking about that dream or vision or whatever it was I had when I was unconscious in the wreck. It haunted me. It had been so real, that was one thing about it, so intense. Not like a dream at all, really. You see, it was a memory, a very clear recollection of a day in my life when I was maybe nine or ten years old, and so vivid it was kind of scary. Like, I had *felt* the sun on my back as I lay once again on the bank— warm and good. I had smelled the mud under my nose, heard the water gurgling away back under the bank. That had been a very happy, a very beautiful day. And it was the same, exactly the same: a total recall of everything that happened that day, right up to the end. Then it changed, and when it changed, that was when that feeling came in, that feeling of frustration or hopelessness or whatever. I don't know how to describe it, but it was really, really bad.

You see, the way it really happened, I didn't run all the way home. I turned around and hollered insults at that guy. And he hollered insults back at me—"Yaaah! you look like your grandmother!" and stuff like that. Indian insults. And I walked home. I even went down to the water, to the lake, and washed my face, because I'd been crying and I didn't want anyone to know that. And my nose was bloody. When I got home I waited for my brothers to get out of school. Then I tried to persuade them to come back over there with me and get my fish, but they wouldn't go. So I went down to Fisher's and tried to get Scotty to go with me. And he wouldn't go, but his brother, Stan, went with me. When we got there, that guy's brothers were home from school too, and they were bigger than we were. So we just turned around and came home. That's what really happened.

Well, I didn't know what to make of that, and I still don't know. But it was a turning point in my life, that I do know. When I went back to work after my holiday that feeling went with me, that cloud I tried to run away from. I'd wake up in the middle of the night, really tired, needing my sleep, and I'd be under that cloud. And now it had all to do with business. The restaurant, the dress shop, the grocery store—the whole thing was just depressing. It kept working on me, pushing me lower and lower. The only way I could deal with it was to go to the reserve or go into the bush. Finally, it just all caved in on me. So I sold everything out and bought a tourist resort.

I went to the bush permanently then, I figured. But see, it was still a business! It wasn't just being in the bush; it was a business. Now the business was hunting and fishing, but it was a business just the same. Like pro ball, it wasn't fun; it was work. And it was making money out of wildlife. Maybe that was the reason I never made it there either.

It was really great up there. When I was running over in the cruiser to pick up guests at the government dock, some days were so nice, so warm, I'd stop on one of the islands and just lie down there on the rocks, and there'd be seagulls hatching out—you know, the little seagulls. And they'd be walking all around there, and they're all brown and small and lopsided and topheavy. And they'd come around and they'd kind of bounce forward—come right around you. Just pull up your boat and lie there on the rocks—it was great! I really loved that life, except that there it was business.

I could have kept that lodge. I was in trouble—had

spent too much on advertising—but not bad trouble. And I knew all about good business practice: how to bear down, cut expenses, and keep afloat. I also had good credit. But that wasn't it. Something else was happening to me —had been happening, I suppose, for a long time. I was going down and down and down in the sense of white values and white goals. It just seemed like there was no way to stop it. I was getting out of all that—that becoming thing—becoming a success, becoming somebody. But I wasn't doing it like a smart white man would, selling out at a profit, if possible, or going into bankruptcy. I was doing it like a dumb Indian. Failing out.

Anyway, I left the whole lodge thing and went to North Bay, to a job cooking in a restaurant. That was my stepping stone to the reserve, I suppose, because I stayed there only three months. Then I went home to Wikwemikong. And I stayed for nearly two years.

4 · Home
Is Here

WE FOUND a little house, Dorrie and I and Jennifer, who was just a baby then. It's gone now, that little shack. It belonged to my aunt, and she is gone now too. It had a kitchen and one other room. It was right next door to the house my dad built, the house I grew up in. There was always a well there in that yard, but never any pump. There was a round pole and a wooden cover, a lid, and we'd drop the pail into the water and then we'd wind it up on that pole. We just had a string on our pail, just a rope. And in winter it was icy around that thing, because it was always dripping, and the pail was always bent and you knocked the hell out of it dropping it down. So we poured into other pails, and it took two to fill another pail.

But there was really something about that whole thing of going back home. It was really a great relief! All that weight I had been packing around, worrying about this, worrying about that . . . worry about all kinds of things, all kinds of things for survival. And suddenly, all that's gone. The tourist resort is gone, the restaurant is gone, the apparel shop is gone, the grocery store is gone, and I'm just back home. And what I remember most about that is the calm. It was like going through a big storm in a little boat and then coming into a harbor where it is calm and peaceful.

When I think about all that—going home to Wikwemikong—what stands out more than anything else is that sense of relief, the sense of shedding a terrific burden. I had been living under pressure, always under pressure. There were always things that had to be done right now, taken care of. And whether I felt like doing them or not didn't matter; they had to be done. And all those things just fell away, and here we were suddenly living in very simple circumstances with people who accepted us totally. And we had nothing.

The day began when we got up. There wasn't any particular time to get up or go to bed, although most of the time we got up early and went to bed early. I suppose that's the way all country people do. We had no TV, we didn't even have a radio, so everything going on in our house was real. We had a woodstove. I didn't have to get up the wood, it was supplied with the rent, but I did have to split it and bring it in. Getting up and lighting the stove every morning and keeping the stove going, keeping the place warm, even a simple thing like that seemed to have a lot of meaning. Of course, we had no running water in the little house. We had to carry water from the well, which wasn't very far; it was just outside the house a ways. The people next door had a washing machine, and Dorrie used to heat all the water and do her washing over next door.

I had no money, no credit. There was no work on the reserve I could make money at. Once again, I was just another damn Indian. I had fallen back into survival, Indian style. What that means is that you work—sometimes you work like hell—but you're not an employee and you don't get paid money. You get paid in a different way— satisfactions, I suppose you'd call them—the good feeling of your body coming together with hard work, the good feeling of your life coming together because all the nonessentials have fallen away and the whole thing is just simple, very simple and primary. There's a direct line between your head and your hands and your belly. Money, the middleman of survival, has been eliminated. Everything you do is directly related to survival: the wood you cut, the water you draw, the garden you plant, the berries you pick, the fish you catch—and that's your life. And that was our life, but not all of it. There was another element in our survival: the people.

Every day somebody would drop in—some woman would drop in and say, "Well, we had this soup last night. If you want it, it's left over. There's enough there for three or four people, but I can't heat it up now because there's eight of us." And there were three of us, so we'd have soup. Or somebody'd drop in with potatoes, or after they'd made bread: "I want you to try my bread." And every day they came. It had nothing to do with them wanting us to try their bread. They were feeding us. And it wasn't just kindness or thoughtfulness, not charity. It was a way of life, of survival. They sustained us because, with Indians, if the community doesn't survive, no one survives. But that's how they would come. They'd sometimes come with a basket; there'd be a loaf of bread in there. And there'd be maybe some fresh pork sausage— somebody had killed a pig, or they'd made blood sausage. We'd open the door and here would be a little girl standing there: "My mother sent this over, she wants you to try this." And maybe there'd be some fresh rolls too. Or a head of lettuce: "That comes from our garden," she'd say. And that's how we lived: people feeding us.

We got our clothes mostly from the rummage sale up at the church. I don't know how many rummage sales they had—one at least every two months, I guess—and Dorrie used to go up to the church and help the ladies sort all the clothes out, lay them out for the sale, put the prices on, and so on. So she would pick out what we needed for ourselves. We got some beautiful clothes for Jennifer for —oh, five cents for this and ten cents for that, very cheap. A lot of those clothes were really very good, very expensive. I don't know where they came from, but I guess they were sent in from other churches or by people in the church who took in clothing and things like that for rummage sales. Later on Dorrie used to work sometimes, used to get as much as two or three days a week teaching in the school as a substitute. My sister Rosemary sometimes did that too. They paid nine dollars a day, and it helped out.

But the money thing was funny around there. You didn't really need any money. People would come along and they'd say, "Come on, we're going over, such and such a place," and you'd say, "Well, I'd like to go but I . . . I don't think I'll go, I haven't got any money." And they'd say, "Aw, come on! You don't need any money, I got lots of money. Come on!" So you'd get your boots on and go with them, and they paid. And you never had to worry about paying them back or anything like that. Of course, if and when you had money something would work out where you'd take them somewhere, and *you'd* pay next time. But it didn't have to be that way.

When we first went to Wikwemikong I did have a car. It wasn't paid for, but I could make a buck now and again just because I had a car. I used to run a sort of taxi service to Manitowaning. And I bootlegged. I'd buy a couple of bottles of whiskey if I had the money, and then I'd sell it for twice the price. Of course, everybody on the reserve bootlegged. Well, maybe not everybody, but a lot of people. And the reason was that people got paid at different times. Sometimes some people would have some money and other people wouldn't have very much, so the people who had money would buy whiskey and sell it to the people who needed it. But then a week or so later the other people would get their pay checks and they'd have some money, so they'd buy booze and sell it back to the people that they bought booze from a couple of weeks before. It all sort of evened out. But they were all bootleggers. And the money just kept going back and forth between all those bootleggers. Being broke, I didn't use much whiskey, but I sold a lot of it. There was a film show once or twice a week at the Hall and out at Kaboni, and I helped on that; I worked at that as projectionist. I'd get, say, three, maybe four dollars a night two or three nights a week doing that.

But my car—you know, I was really hiding from the finance company because I didn't have any money for the payments, so I'd always park it in a different place. I kept a jump ahead of them that way. But then one of my brothers decided to borrow some gears out of the rear end of it. I wasn't able to move it around any more, so one day they came and got it. Then I was cleaned; didn't even have a car any more. But by then it was on the blink anyway, so I really didn't care. I didn't miss it. I didn't feel sad about them taking it. I suppose it was really the last link with our previous life, Dorrie's and mine, out there in the business world.

I felt freer when that car was gone, and we began to

find that it made a big difference to our way of life. Now there were all kinds of places we couldn't go, or that we would get to very seldom because it was too far to walk. We could only go to those places close enough to walk to. Our experience of the community began to be a walking experience. The whole pace of our lives slowed down to walking speed. Wikwemikong is a hilly place, so wherever we went we climbed hills up and down, and sometimes we'd stop halfway up a hill to catch our breath, and it was great just looking around while we stood there, down on the village below us. We became aware of all kinds of things like clouds and wind and all the sounds of the village. We got to know all the dogs, and we began to get to know those people who lived nearest us much, much better. I don't know whether the car had anything to do with it—it may be that Dorrie and I were home more— anyway, the teen-age kids in the community began to come to our place. Our place always seemed to have lots of young people in it. Jennifer was a little baby, and young girls would pick her up and take her out in her carriage or in her little sled almost every day. We had a big crib-bage tournament going in that house most of the winter. We taught all those kids to play cribbage and when they got good enough, we had a cribbage tournament.

And I got to playing hockey. I wasn't in very good shape, but I got back so I could skate and that was really good for me. I'd go down and play hockey with the guys in the rink. I coached a kids' team throughout the winter and I played a lot of badminton.

Maybe the thing that distinguishes Indian reserves (and all rural communities, I guess) from the city is that you know everybody. Everything is personal. Living in Wikwemikong, I'd look out the window and whoever I saw going by it was always someone I knew. The thought would pass through my head: Oh, there's old Emile; he's going to the store. Or I might see Sarah and I could be pretty sure she was going to visit Genevieve.

I realize that many urban people might feel they would resent this kind of intimacy. Some might even see it as a kind of spying—an invasion of privacy—but it was a very practical aspect of community life. I remember old Francis, for example, going past our house every morning, carrying a two-quart tin pail. The pail was painted red. Francis lived all alone, and everyone knew he was on his way to Odjig's to get his daily supply of milk. One morning we saw Sarah, the little girl who lived next door to Francis, carrying Francis' pail. Everyone on the route from Francis' house to Odjig's was wondering, just as we were, what had happened to Francis.

On her way back from Odjig's, Sarah was stopped by several people, including me, all inquiring about Francis. We learned he was sick in bed. Some people sent messages with Sarah. Soon someone arrived at Francis' house with some hot broth. Someone else cleaned up his house and fed the chickens. Another brought herbs and began brewing a healing tea. A guy who played cribbage came with his crib board and cards. That night someone stayed with Francis and kept the stove well stoked with wood. And so, without any fuss or overlap or conscious effort to organize, Francis was taken care of, until once again we saw him going past our door in the morning, little red pail in hand.

I had to go in to Toronto one time when I was living there on the reserve. A whole carload of us went and I took a young niece of mine along; she was about eleven or twelve and had never been to the city. So we were walking along one of the main downtown streets and I was busily pointing out all the sights, and of course, there were hundreds of people on the streets. We came to a stop light and stood, waiting for the light to change. So I took this opportunity to point out yet another urban wonder. "See," I said, "this is a completely automatic light. Instead of having to have a policeman here to tell people when to cross the street, this light tells them. It comes on red and then after a certain time it just switches over to green and then the people know it is safe to walk." And she said, "But where are they going?"

Well, that little incident sort of blew my mind and got me thinking about that whole thing. By knowing everyone on the reserve, I don't just mean I knew their names. If you live in a reserve community you don't just know people's names; you also know who their parents were, and their grandparents. And there was often a lot more to it than that. When I saw Joe Fisher, for example, I knew his real name wasn't Fisher, it was Oskaboose. He went by the name of Fisher only because his mother died when he was an infant and he was taken and raised by George and Grace Fisher. And the Fishers were really Odjigs. (*Odjig* is the Indian name for "fisher," a valuable fur-bearing animal. Some of the Odjig clan went by the English name Fisher; some stuck to Odjig.)

If a man was having a hard time financially, it was quite common for someone in better circumstances to offer to take one of that man's kids and raise it as one of his own. So the child would have two sets of parents, and usually he'd end up with the name of his adopted parents just through usage. Of course, the child was free to stay where he chose, and often he would live with one set of parents for a while and then go home to the others. Either way, he went home. There were no "illegitimate" children on the reserve except in the church records. A child born to an unmarried mother usually fitted into that girl's family circle in a totally acceptable way. And even if the girl happened to be in circumstances that made it difficult for her to keep and look after the child herself, her parents or grandparents were always glad to have the child. There were always lots of people eager to adopt and look after children.

I have a few friends in Sault Sainte Marie, good friends who have asked me, "Wilf, after you left here and went back on the reserve, what the hell did you do for those two years?" I don't know why they ask that question. Maybe it's just curiosity, maybe they have some funny ideas about reserves—I don't know. But I find that a very difficult question to answer even to my own satisfaction. Reserve life, for most, is not routine. And I suppose to a lot of people, that means you don't do anything. But I was active, active as hell. Not much is planned, that's true, but something's always happening. Like, one thing that really stands out in my memory is laughter, and one thing laughter means is fun: good times and good people. It seems to me that my days were filled with laughter, and that was pretty different from what I had been experiencing. My days in business had been filled with seriousness and very little laughter, and I began to realize how much I had missed laughter and how important it is, how it enriches your life to laugh every day. I can't remember either that the conversation got into serious subjects very much, like politics or education or religion or any of those things that people out there talk about so much. And of course we went to lots of parties, and those parties were Indian style —you know, everyone was there. They weren't parties for old people or young people or middle-aged people or any particular group; everyone was there, the young and the old. I had forgotten what that felt like, too.

And I used to go with old Joe Peltier sometimes on the mail route, just to keep him company and because I enjoyed being with him. He was a cousin of mine and had the same name as my grandfather. The driver of the mail truck performed a dual service because the mail truck was also a sort of unofficial bus. There were always people along the road who knew the mail truck would be coming and they would want a ride here or a ride there, a ride into town, so we would never go very far before the truck was full of people—mostly old people. One time when I went with him the truck got so full of people that I got off in Kaboni, which is a way out from Wikwemikong, and I said to him, "Now, I'll be along the road here someplace and you can pick me up on the way back." But when he came back he had even more people with him, so he went right on and left me to get home as best I could. So I spent the day visiting around with people and with friends I had there and I got a ride home okay. There was never any problem; you never had to worry about getting home because there was usually someone going in that direction, and if there wasn't, there were all kinds of people you could stay with overnight. I often think about that when I'm hurrying down the street to move my car because I'm afraid I'm going to get a ticket. I don't chase buses any more, but there have been times when I have, and that would flash through my mind; then I would always stop chasing the bus and all that anxiety about catching it would disappear because I would start laughing about the whole situation, laughing at myself.

I remember one time when Joe Peltier dropped in in

the evening as he was always doing. Dorrie at that time just happened to be weaning Jennifer off the bottle and she was fretting about it, wouldn't go to sleep in her crib. And when he left he didn't say anything, but he picked up Dorrie's cigarettes and took them with him. And that was his way of telling her, of saying, "Well, how do you like it when people take something you like away from you? Something that you're accustomed to having."

When I first went back to the reserve I guess I was nervous about how I might be received. And that's the measure of how much I'd forgotten. You see, I'd almost made it out there in that white community and I thought, Jesus, you know, somebody's going to say to me . . . well, we have a word, *kichmendesuh*, which means "he likes himself" or "he thinks he's better than the rest of us." It's our word for being stuck-up. But nobody saw any manager or restaurant owner or lodge operator or any of those things; they just saw Wilf Pelletier. And I can't tell you how beautiful that was. I was just accepted. They knew all about me—what I had been doing in the Sault—all that. And going broke. Everything. But nobody ever asked about my background or what happened or anything. There was just me there, and I just fit in the community. That whole feeling was pretty nice. I was just there, and I was accepted.

Well, I learned something from all that about myself. I got a look at Wilf Pelletier; saw, really saw what he had been doing to himself all those years out there, working so hard, striving to become a success, to become somebody —and putting himself down. Denying the somebody he really was. And I saw how I got sucked into all that too. Out there you can't get by just as a person. There was very little room for Indians out there, that was for sure. And

Wilf Pelletier . . . it wasn't good enough to be just Wilf Pelletier, no matter how you spelled the name. You had to be Wilf Pelletier, Restaurateur, or Wilf Pelletier, Lodge Owner. And I bought all that bullshit. I went for it, hook, line, and sinker.

Yet here I was back home, broke, being fed by my kinfolk. With no identity except just me, Wilf Pelletier. I didn't think of myself as anything, not even Indian. The people all around me were something classified as Indian, but I didn't feel any need to be Indian or to be anything but Wilf Pelletier. But, oh God, how I needed to be me! How I needed to let that poor bastard I had been stomping down for so long get free and sort of come to the surface again so I could get to know him.

And they did that for me, the people of that community. Because that was the only Wilf Pelletier they knew or could recognize—the real one. So that happened to me: I met Wilf Pelletier once again; got pretty well acquainted with him. And I liked what I saw. I recognized that he was Indian, that he would never be anything but Indian, and he'd better accept that and do something with it instead of trying to get around it.

I guess that's when I knew I would be going back out there into mainstream society. I didn't know when and I didn't know what I'd be doing out there, but I knew, whatever it turned out to be, the guy doing it would be just Wilf Pelletier.

The other part of that whole thing that happened to me was that I sort of got to know my own people. And that's kind of hard to explain because I don't mean I related to them in a different or better way. I'm not talking about relationships. I mean I began to understand them better and appreciate them more. I found I was observing all sorts of behavior, the behavior of my own people. I was very conscious of that because I'd been out in the white world and I was quite familiar with the way things were done out there and the way people behaved. And I found that people behaved quite differently on the reserve. There were many, many little things that were very different, so many of them exactly opposite to the sorts of things that were done in that world out there. I didn't have any answers at that time for those differences and they puzzled me. But I could see that the values were different. The Indian community was not moralistic, and I guess one of the results was that the behavior generally was much more spontaneous, much freer, more honest. And the more I watched, the more my respect for Indian people and the Indian view of life went up. For one thing, they weren't into playing games in their relationships. Teasing, yes, the kind that always led to a lot of fun and laughter. But not those dead-serious games where some-body wins and somebody loses.

It wasn't just the people of the community, either, that I was aware of. There were also the people coming home, some just for weekends or holidays. People who had jobs outside somewhere, in Detroit or Toronto or North Bay or maybe Sudbury, they would come home. And school kids, youngsters away at residential school, they came home in the summer. And I watched all that: how they talked too much, laughed too loud. How active they were, running all over, trying to be everyplace at once. And how, after a few days, they began to quiet down and behave like the rest of the people instead of like whites. And I used to wonder about that. Every year, hundreds of Indian kids going to the city. Why did they ever leave the reserve? Of course, *I* was the exception, I knew why

I had to go, but the others? After all, what was so attractive about that hostile world out there?

For every Indian kid living on the reserve that city, that white world, is always out there and I don't really know what it all means to those kids. It means money, I suppose, but then I don't think they value money the way whites do. My impression is that they don't treat it the same way. Maybe the city is attractive to them in the sense of an excursion they'd like to take and then come back. I sometimes think that none of those kids ever go out into urban society the first time with any intention of staying there. It's challenge, I guess—you know, to be able to go out and stay out there a while and then come back and act like a man of the world, like someone who really knows his way around.

But what makes me think that none of them ever looks on the city as home or ever intends to stay there is that they are always wanting to go home, always talking about getting home. And they do go home as often as they can manage to do it. Lots of them spend all their money just traveling back and forth. And home, of course, is the reserve. It isn't just a family they go to or a house, it's a whole community. I have tried to observe my own feelings many times—I still do—coming back to the reserve, and the strongest part of that whole feeling is that I've come home. That's such a great feeling. I've come home.

When you go to Wikwemikong the last town you go through is the little village of Manitowaning. From there on the road is gravel. You drive about nine miles and quite suddenly you come over a little rise, and there, down below you, is the village of Wikwemikong. Right there at that little rise there's a big rock and a cross standing: that marks the boundary of the village. Sometimes I come at night. At night the lights are all winking away down below there. Sometimes I come in the daytime and I can see the Bay stretching away, blue to the horizon, and the little village sitting on the side of the Bay. I always stop the car there and I get out and I holler. I holler as loud as I can holler. And maybe I'll let out half a dozen war whoops. Now, I don't know why I do that. I think maybe it might be a symbol of some kind, but it really feels great; it feels free, it feels great! I can't do that in the white community. No matter how much I feel like hollering, if I'm in downtown Toronto, I can't, because it will attract a lot of attention and the police will come or the men in white coats and something will have to be done about this very strange behavior.

Then I take a piss. And I don't know why I do that either, except I usually need to. But maybe that's a sort of symbol too. Freedom. Out there, I've got to use a toilet. Here, I can piss anywhere, anytime. I've been pissing all over this reserve since I was a little boy. And as I stand there, taking a piss and looking down on the village—I don't know just how to say this—but it's like I embrace that whole place, every house in it, every individual in every house, and I feel that they embrace me, they include me totally. They accept me totally and I accept them totally.

I guess part of that is coming from a hypocritical world, where people are under pressure to perform in a way they think will win approval or think will be acceptable, into a community where none of that exists, where you don't have to do any of that, where the people accept each other for what they are, not for the performance they are able to give. And that's a very great freedom and a very great responsibility. Another way of saying it, I suppose, is that you come from the world of doing into a community of being, where people do things but the things they do are not deeds, they're only a reflection of what they are. Doing is being. What you do is never a performance, a role you play, because that's not only unnecessary, it's grotesque.

I've come home dozens of times, hundreds of times, and no one has ever asked me where I came from or what I'm doing now or where I'm living now or how much money I make or what sort of job I have or any of these questions which are so common in white society. What that means is that the people in that community don't place any importance on these things. They like me and love me as I like and love them, and when I come home they are happy to see me and they don't see anyone except Wilf, who was once a little boy and who's now older and bigger and a man, but who is still Wilf, really unchanged. I haven't become anything, I'm not somebody; I'm just who I always was—Wilf. I don't have to account for myself, I don't have to impress anyone, I don't have to explain myself, I don't have to do anything. I'm allowed just to be, and that is the greatest freedom I know. That is what I mean when I say I've come home. And that is life, total life. And that is the world. There isn't anything outside of that.

Yeah, that's all there is except that one other thing, and that one other thing—I don't know what it is. It can be called "the job," or I guess it could be given lots of names. Anyway, there are hundreds of Indian people like me who go home, but only for a few days, a weekend or whatever, and then they go back to that job. They're a toolmaker or a student or a factory worker or something; they leave and go back to that job. Even though the reserve is all there

is. And I don't know . . . oh, I can talk about economic
necessity, the need to survive and so on, and there aren't
any jobs on the reserve so you have to go outside to find
a job. All that. But I know that doesn't explain it. You're
damned if you do and damned if you don't. Everyone has
to decide for himself what poverty is, what survival is—
to be rich in relationships and poor in possessions, or the
other way around. For Indians, it seems to be a choice
between staying home and having very little (which is
really everything) and going away in order to achieve
relative affluence (which is nothing). I do know that the
whole thing I'm talking about of going home, that's what
religion is all about. Those people want to go home, all the
people in the world. And I wonder . . . I don't think there
are very many who get home any more through organized
religion because the people who are trying to lead the way
don't know where they're going. What I mean by going
home is finding your own people—not just your blood
relations, your *whole* family, wherever they may be anywhere in the world. And I guess that means recognition:
knowing the members of your family at a glance and
having them know you. People who accept you without
question. Because if your medium of exchange is not love,
you can't survive.

5·The
Indian Business

◻▭◻▭◻▭◻▭◻▭◻

WHEN I LEFT the reserve after two years I came to
Toronto, and I suppose I thought about that as starting all
over again. I had been out there in mainstream society
once and had cut quite a swath in the business world, and
had finally ended up back on the reserve with nothing.
Now I was starting all over again.

When I first went to the city I went alone; I went on
ahead of Dorrie. I stayed with a cousin of mine who lived
out in a suburb. I would go looking for a job all day in
Toronto. I didn't have any money and sometimes I would
have to walk back out to where he lived, which was a long
way. It used to take me four, five hours to walk that
distance; I guess it was nine or ten miles.

Finally, I got a job as a handyman. It wasn't much of
a job. I was paid forty or fifty dollars a week, something
like that. I cleaned up rooms, made beds, looked after the
gardens, and fixed anything that needed fixing. And all
that other experience, my business experience, was behind me. Sometimes, when I was making beds or mopping
out rooms, I would think, Goddammit, Wilfred, you almost made it! You almost made it! But I didn't really know

what I meant when I said that to myself. All I knew—all I can say about it now—is that somehow or other that whole thing had something to do with being Indian. This time there would be no denial of my racial identity, that much I knew. But how to make it as Wilf Pelletier, Indian, was beyond me.

Dorrie and I found a little furnished apartment. It really wasn't much of a place, a basement apartment with pipes running along the ceilings—in fact, when you came in the door you had to duck your head to keep from hitting it on a pipe. And when it got warmed up in there the moisture would condense on the pipes and start dripping all over. The place was equipped with inside weather. We didn't have any windows, so it was always night unless you pushed a switch and turned the sun on. It was kind of nice except for the built-in rain—I didn't like that. There was one bedroom; we had a bed in there for Jennifer. Dorrie and I had a chesterfield that pulled out into a bed in the living room. That's where we slept. Dorrie managed to get a part-time job at twenty-five dollars a week, and that helped out.

It was a big change from the reserve, where we hadn't any particular need of money. We found that in the city there was no way you could survive without money. I remember one time when my mother was staying with us and she was very, very ill. We had to get an ambulance to move her down to the hospital. We didn't have any money, she didn't have any money, and we had to have eighteen dollars to pay for the ambulance or they wouldn't come. Finally Dorrie phoned up an Indian friend of ours and within ten minutes there was an ambulance at the door. But it was frightening, and sometimes you felt very helpless. Except for one priest who gave me a job, there were only two or three Indian people who would help us. Not many Indians had the means to help someone else.

I wasn't able to find steady employment. I worked here and there at odd jobs, but eventually even that ran out and we found ourselves really up against it, so I applied for welfare. And that was quite an experience. I think I got something like twenty-two dollars out of it, but in order to get that I had to go through things I would just never go through again. I would never do that. I was supposed to report back there next week—I suppose to get more welfare, I don't know. And I did go back, and I stood across the street and looked at that welfare office and I couldn't make myself go any closer than that. There was no way that I could force myself to go in and go through that experience again. I would have starved first.

I guess that was one of the lowest points in my life. Everything went out the window in order to get that twenty-two bucks. You know, the whole process by which I got it made me feel so low, and it was impressed on me so deeply by those people that everything was my fault and that I really needed help. Yet there they were working and drawing their pay checks, and it seemed to me that they should have been satisfied with that. They should have accepted me as a person who needed help temporarily. Because if I wasn't coming in there for help, they wouldn't have any jobs.

That low point was when I first started getting riled up about the Indian thing. I came out of that experience of trying to find a job and having to apply for welfare feeling, Goddammit, you know, all this land was Indian land and you're all a bunch of foreigners and land grabbers and thieves, and what's this you're putting me through here anyway? After all, if anyone belongs in this land, I do. And I guess that was when I began to know who I was, and accept who I was, and respect who I was. Anyway, one of the first things I did in Toronto was join the Indian Club.

When I talk about losing my people, what I mean more than anything else is what happens to you when you get into becoming an Indian. That's a pretty crazy trip. How can you become something or someone when that's what you are already? I didn't know I was doing that, but I had the idea that in order to be Indian you had to know all about Indians everywhere and you had to be able to do all the things that Indians do, like dancing and so on. I can even remember going home on weekends, going home to Wikwemikong, and coming away feeling that I knew a lot more about Indians than my own people did. What I didn't realize was that I was consciously trying to become what they quite unconsciously were.

I don't know how you would describe that condition. Disassociation, maybe. Anyhow, I got involved in teaching Indian dancing because I thought Indians in the city should be occupied with Indian activities. I guess the people in that Indian club weren't becoming Indians fast enough to suit me. I really didn't know anything about Indian dancing, except I'd been to a couple of powwows, but I went ahead anyhow. Well, it caught on and everyone was into making costumes and practicing dancing. Sometimes we even had big feeds of corn soup and bannock, both of which are distinctive Indian foods.

I don't know how it happened, but right about then I got an invitation from the Indian club in Winnipeg to come and teach Indian dancing. They offered to pay my way. Well, I knew that those people out there, some of them anyway, really knew how to dance. Some of them had been to all kinds of powwows. So I was pretty scared about that. But I went anyway. I didn't teach anything while I was there, but I learned something, and it was something I think I'd always known. I learned that you can't teach Indian dancing.

When I got there I found a big crowd of people had assembled in this hall. I don't know what they expected but I just asked, "Have you got a drum?" And they said, "Yes, but we don't have any singers." So I said, "That's okay, just bring the drum out and put it in the middle of the floor." Then I got out there and I sang one song. When I finished, a guy came along, took the drumstick, and began very softly beating on the drum. I knew right away he was a singer, just the way he hit that drum. Then another came along and another, and pretty soon there were singers all around the drum. And it was happening. People just got up and started dancing. And that's how I taught Indian dancing in Winnipeg.

When I came back to Toronto I told everyone that you can't teach Indian dancing, you just get up and do it. And that from watching other people and just doing it, you learn the steps and the beat. I told them you just dance how you feel, and that's the essence of Indian dancing. But you've got to learn it on your own and do it on your own.

Eventually we developed a group of dancers and we got to be pretty good. We began to be well known, so that we'd get asked to dance professionally. And we did some of that here and there, and the money was good. But more and more, even though we knew we could exploit our popularity, become really successful, and probably make a lot of money, we felt that what we were doing was not really ours to sell. It belonged to the people as a whole, the Indian people. And we wanted to give it to them. So we found ourselves being invited and going to various Indian communities. And what we really looked forward to was being fed there. A big feast, that was our pay, and we valued it above money. It wasn't the food, although we all enjoyed eating; it was the whole way we were received by those people who saw our dancing. It was the prospect of good company and fun and laughter, which I guess all Indian people associate with food. So really, we were not a professional troup of entertainers. We were just some young guys who were enjoying what we were doing and learning, I guess, learning more and more about ourselves in the process.

I can only speak for myself, but I think that the whole Toronto thing—that whole trip—was an attempt to find our way home, to discover ourselves as Indians, and the dance thing was the beginning of it. But for my part, I was still badly mixed up. On the one hand, I enjoyed being accepted as an Indian. I had never had any experience of that before in the white community, and now here I was, going out dancing, and whites were applauding and demonstrating that they appreciated something Indian. I liked that. On the other hand, I was really mad, I was really angry. I was determined I was going to shove that whole thing of Indian inferiority down the white man's throat, that I was going to beat them at their own game. And so I set out to do that.

But that was hard, really difficult, because it seemed I was always being defeated by my own people. Part of that disassociation—losing sight of my people—was seeing them as problems. Indians were problems: that was the white consensus, and it was hard to argue with. Indians were poor, Indians were unemployed, Indians were al-coholic—all misfits and failures. Well, I was Indian and I was determined to come to grips with the Indian problem and force the whites to realize Indians were capable of any achievement if given half a chance, although I wasn't at all sure how to do that.

But I had lots of white advisers, and the commonest advice I got was, Get involved. Get more of your people involved. All kinds of people said that. What those people were really talking about was organization. What they really meant to say was, Build an Indian organization. That was hard for me to understand, because in an Indian community you don't *get* involved, you *are* involved. But you aren't organized. And those urban Indians were in-volved in the life of the city, but they weren't organized. But even though I didn't understand what involvement meant, I tried anyhow. I even rounded up Indians and wangled things so they'd show up at a dinner or a meet-ing. And they did show up a few times, but then they got on to me—began to realize I was manipulating them. Then I began to lose all my friends. After that I would arrange a meeting with influential whites, and no Indians would show up. I'd ask a reliable Indian friend to take some small responsibility, and never see him again. It was frustrating, but that same frustration, though I didn't realize it then, was my excuse for becoming a professional Indian helper. The only question left for me was how best to do that.

One thing I had noticed even during my business days in the Sault was that organizations command more re-spect than individuals. At meetings, it seemed to me, peo-ple were always being asked, "What organization do you represent?" In fact, most people would announce that, would preface their remarks with a statement of what they belonged to, so it seemed logical to me that the more organizations you were in, the more people would respect you. So I began joining organizations—I went on an organization orgy. It was easy because many organizations wanted at least one Indian and there was considerable rivalry between them to get Indians. You'd even hear talk like, "Oh, we've got an educated Indian. He's got grade twelve," or, "He's going to university," and so on. So it was a two-way street: Indians who sought to use organizations were being used by organizations. And that's still going on today.

I got on the Social Planning Council and various committees in that. I joined the Canadian Folk Art Council, and they had all kinds of committees also. I was active on some of those. That Canadian Folk Art Council was just formed, and it was the mayor's baby. We used to go down to the mayor's office sometimes to meet, so I got to know the mayor and all the city officials, and I got to know the heads of all the other ethnic groups in Toronto. Some of these people were what you might call the big shots and were looked up to by a particular racial segment as a sort of granddaddy because they were members of the Philharmonic or something like that. And others had made a success in business and had lots of money. Also, I got asked to appear on radio—the CBC—and television, just through moving around with all these people. I also became involved with citizenship organizations and various women's groups. And I began to learn what was going on. Throughout that time of meetings, going to countless meetings, I hardly ever said a word. Never spoke in public. For nearly five years I just listened and observed what people were doing.

Meantime I was still in the Indian Club and after a while I was elected president. I guess I wasn't a very good president because I never did anything. That wasn't entirely due to laziness. From my observation of many organizations I was convinced that when the executive attempts to control everything and do everything, none of the people in the organization get involved. So the place was busy as an anthill. Everybody seemed to be into something and things got done. I did take the initiative in attempting to get a building for the Indian Club. I had become convinced, from attending many meetings and from long hours of listening, that it was just not possible for Indian people to achieve things like raising money and acquiring buildings and so on without enlisting the help of influential whites. [So that's what happened with all that thing of getting a building.] And we did succeed eventually, although this came about after I had resigned as president. But the Indian Club didn't get the building. A new entity, the Indian Centre, had been created, and it got the building. The Indian Club died.

What happened was that the sympathetic whites who started out to help us Indians ended up on the Indian Centre directorate. They ran it; the Indian Centre was white-directed. It was also politically oriented. So that hardly knowing how it happened, the Indians were suddenly into politics. The Indian Centre stayed that way for a long time. It was seven or eight years before an Indian became president, and longer than that before it employed an Indian director. Throughout that time a variety of whites used that club to fill their own needs—the need of a cause to promote which would make them feel good.

I have mixed feelings about Indian centers as such because my impression of them generally, throughout

Canada and the United States, is that they do serve a useful purpose for some urban Indians. Some Indians go there regularly. On the other hand, the vast majority of urban Indians are not attracted to the local center—never go near it. It is my feeling that this is so because most Indian people shy away from involvement in the structured activities and heavy programming which tend, inevitably, to turn Indians into statistics. They prefer to do their own thing.

I think that's the most depressing experience Indians have—being put through by the do-gooders, the professional hypocrites. And finding that all the Indian organizations are controlled by these people, the people who want to use Indians. I don't think I was ever bitter about that whole Indian putdown when I was guiding, but as I got more involved in Western society—in mainstream organizations—I found that I couldn't get on the executive because I was Indian. That got to me. I found I could be a member—member at large or something. That's all. But I could never hold an executive position.

This bitter experience led some of us to the conclusion that you just couldn't work with whites. They always ended up in the driver's seat. How far we were at that time from understanding why that was so is indicated by our firm belief that we had to get some power, some influence, somehow. We had to be heard. So we decided to start an all-Indian newspaper. We called it *The Thunderbird*, and depending on your point of view, I guess it had some success. Four or five people became involved in writing and editing—producing the paper—and they learned something from that. During the three to four years we published that paper quite a number of people worked on it, and I think all of them enjoyed it.

Since the great majority of our readers were white we slanted our paper in their direction, hoping to activate some of them and use white influence to put pressure on government. Get some action for Indians, that was the idea, because Indians didn't seem to be able to do that by their own efforts. Our primary editorial target was government, particularly the Department of Indian Affairs, and since government screwed things up every time they went anywhere near Indians, we always had plenty of material. We had articles on police brutality—the Mounties using dogs on Indians in Saskatchewan; articles on poverty, on pollution, on the flooding of Indian lands. Anything political: it was a whole political trip.

Looking back on all that, I can see we didn't have any particular feeling for those Indians, we wrote about, no personal awareness of what they were going through. We identified with them racially but not personally. We didn't identify with their suffering. Had they been white instead of Indian, it is even possible we would have got some pleasure out of their difficulties.

But one thing we didn't allow for was the number of do-gooders in society. We'd do a story on poverty, maybe print a letter from some old guy up north just as it came to us. Then letters would pour in—people wanting to help. What can we do, and so on. We were snowed under. The first thing we knew clothing depots were being established; quantities of food were being shipped up to those northern communities. But what food! Canned peaches and pressurized whipped cream. Indians were getting sick all over the place.

Incidents of this kind finally forced us to question the whole newspaper effort. We thought we were performing a real service, but we weren't; we were doing a lot of harm. At least, that's my opinion now. We were speaking for all Indians without consultation, lumping them all together, writing about an abstract thing called Indians. Everything we published enhanced the "problem" stereotype. And I think all the "solutions" we stimulated in white minds had the effect of assimilating Indians.

My protective feelings about Indian culture are not merely sentimental. My real concern is survival—human survival. And preserving the Indian way is preserving a survival pattern which has never depended on destruction. Few people realize how fragile an Indian community is, how difficult it is to help those people without damaging them. And I sometimes think that well-intentioned Indians, Indian do-gooders, politically ambitious Indians, are the worst culprits in this regard. I think the last three or four generations of Indian people—there's an overlap there—will go down in history as those who did more to assimilate their people into white society than any other group of Indians. I have the impression that the younger Indians coming on now are seeing through all that, but I really don't know yet.

In the old days no Indian ever became a politician. Indians didn't get into organizations. Almost all of them were illiterate and they followed the old ways. Few of them ever left the reserve or saw anything of the world, so they didn't get into the white scene. My guess is that those first generations of reservation Indians must have felt defeated. But I don't think they felt inferior. The people of my grandfather's time and my father's generation were the ones who began to really feel that. Began to feel the loss of self-determination, to feel kept, to feel hopeless; began to get desperate. It is only in the last fifty years, with the overwhelming growth of technology, that the impact of white "superiority" has really hit the reserves. With it, the pressure on Indians to copy the features and patterns of white culture has multiplied many times. So it has been inevitable, I suppose, that increasing numbers of Indians feel that the adoption of white values and the white view of life is the only way left to survival.

What modern Indians have to cope with is inferiority, and that feeling is not only a racial heritage, it's also engendered by the experience of growing up on a reserve. To those who live there the reserve has many of the aspects of a game refuge, an area set aside by whites for the preservation of animals. And the presence of white institutions within that preserve makes it certain that every one of those animals will be made aware of his "bestial" characteristics, of the nature of his inferiority. The school on the reserve, if there is one, is not the same as the school in a white town. The school is not there merely to educate; its primary purpose is to civilize. Just so with the church. In a white setting the church provides religious services for those who want them. On an Indian reserve, the objective of the church is to convert the heathen—to Christianize—and great pressure is exerted to convert everyone and see that they attend Mass.

Although I doubt that many of them realize it, those who leave the reserve and make it out there in the city are proving to the dominant society that *this* Indian is not an animal, this Indian no longer needs to be "kept" within the refuge, this Indian is civilized. I think that is why a few of the people of my grandfather's generation, some of my father's generation, and many of my own generation became infatuated with organization, with playing the organization game. Became infatuated with the vertical structures of Western European economics and politics.

So some very strange things have happened in the guise of Indian organizations.

I was in the National Indian Council at one time, for example, and it was highly regarded by the white community as a fine Indian organization. Also, those of us who were on the executive were highly regarded by the white community as Indian leaders. The truth is that we weren't representative of the real people at all; we were just some sick Indians on a political trip. Our organization was not Indian, not in the Indian tradition; it was in the white tradition, and of course it was pleasing to whites because what they saw in it was a reflection of themselves and their own culture. The same thing was true of the Indian Club in Toronto. It was made up of Indians, but it was really a white organization, vertical in structure. All its activities were carried on after the white pattern.

Today there are more and more Indian reserves where they have a band office, and that's highly organized—it's like city hall on the reserve. In the old days, if you wanted to see the chief you took your shotgun and went and called on him and maybe went out shooting ducks for a couple of hours in the morning, and by the time you got back you had sort of finished your business with him. Or you called on him in the evening. Nowadays you can't even do that. You go to the band office and a pretty young Indian girl receptionist says to you, "What can I do for you?" And you say you want to see the chief, and she makes an appointment for you. You have to have an appointment to see him, and if you go to see him in the evening, that's a social call. There's no way you're going to do any business then. You have to do business in his office.

That's happening on many reserves, and one of the results is that the chief and council are being isolated from the people because the old way of communication is now blocked. Another result is that the people who are elected to office—the chief and council—live in a kind of organizational dream world. Not having any realistic day-to-day contact with the people on the reserve any more, they really don't know what's going on. And they get more and more into running the reserve according to some kind of ideal pattern in their heads—which is not an Indian pattern, it's a white pattern—instead of on the basis of what the people are really thinking and feeling and what they really want. In many cases, on those highly organized reserves where they have a city hall, the chief and council have been sucked into the white approach to administration as a problem-and-solution rationale. They've bought the white view of the Indian community as a problem— Indians as problems—and now they're attacking those problems, whereas a generation or two ago only Indian Affairs attempted to attack those problems.

In retrospect, the saddest period in Indian history may prove to be other than the decade that ended at Wounded Knee. It may turn out to be the period we are passing through at the present time. This will be remembered as the political period, the time when an entire generation of Indians all over the continent became skillful enough at the game of politics to play it in competition with whites. I say that as an old, experienced political gamester.

Although Indian politics has damaged and destroyed an untold number of people and will continue to do so for a while yet, I am at peace with it because I know political involvement was inevitable, and I also know it is a passing phase in Indian experience. It won't last because it can never be made to fit into the Indian way. In addition, I see increasing numbers of young Indians who refuse to have anything to do with politics. When I talk with them, they say politics divides the people and creates minority groups. They tell me there is no such thing as majorities and minorities—there's only people.

Some years ago the Federal Department of Fisheries decided to reduce the commercial catch in certain freshwater Canadian inland lakes. The means they chose was to put a limitation on the number of commercial fishing licenses issued in each area. For one Indian community in northern Manitoba, the result was that forty-nine licenses were available for fifty-two fishermen. At a meeting held by the Indian fishermen, concern centered around the fact that three of their number would not be allowed to fish. To them it didn't matter which three, and there was certainly no competitive scramble for the forty-nine licenses. The solution was found in the age-old pattern of sharing. In short, all fifty-two men behaved as if none were licensed.

That is not the political way. It is the Indian way. And in many communities, it has been suffering a decline. But it isn't dead. And it will come back. I don't know what the answer is, but I do know that every time the Indian people approach government and ask for or demand more freedom, they end up with less freedom. They end up more boxed in than they were formerly, and this is because they are drawn further into the system; they become more a part of the establishment. I don't think the Indian politicians who instigate this kind of thing realize what they're doing. They think they're doing something good for their people, when the result of their efforts is usually just the opposite. They don't seem to see that freedom is not something government can give you. Government doesn't have it, you have it, and when you realize this you exercise it responsibly. If you don't realize it, then you get into things like asking government to give it to you.

Spelled out, what that means to me is that there never will be any such thing as self-determination without self-sufficiency. There never has been. Administering government handouts is a make-believe kind of freedom. Whoever pays the piper calls the tune, and the tune is assimilation. But there is an alternative even though most people, including Indians, would still regard it as insane. Nevertheless, someday soon, somewhere in Canada, some Indian reserve is going to declare its sovereignty; going to start feeling its way toward independence, toward its own version of freedom, its own laws, its own means of keeping the peace, its own answer to survival. Others will follow, and each will make that rediscovery in its own way. Then we'll find out what the Canadian people really think about Indians—and about human rights.

I can't criticize my brothers who've unknowingly done things that are damaging to their own people. I'm as guilty as anyone and I can't question their intentions. So none of this is criticism; it's just an attempt to describe what I think happens. After all, that's the only way you learn, by going through it. And you can go along for years, working like hell, trying to help your people, before you wake up to what's really going on. I suppose there are some who never wake up, but if you're lucky something happens to you. Maybe you hear someone saying something, and it can be something you've heard many times, but this time you really hear it. I'd been in the Indian business in Toronto for several years and was getting quite proficient at it when that happened to me.

"You know, Wilf, you're Indian, why don't you really try to help your people; try to bring them up to your

level?" That's what I heard. All kinds of whites had said
that to me before, but this time it hit me like a ton of bricks
and I thought, What the hell is going on? Bring them up
to my level! What are they trying to do to me?

"Just get more of your people in Toronto here and
bring them up to your level. Then they won't have any
more of these problems." Who were these people? Always
talking about Indians pulling themselves up by their boot-
straps—tiresome crap like, "My grandparents worked
very hard and they tilled the soil . . ." That whole pioneer
circus about the Great Society. And that guy's grandparents probably hadn't even left Europe.

That's when it hit me. Boy, and it hit me solid. Son of
a bitch, I'd done it again! Denied my true identity, this
time by trying to make an exception of myself. I was
Indian, but I wasn't a problem. All those other Indians
were problems—drunks, bums, ignorant—and I was going to help them. That's how I'd been seeing myself.
That's what I'd been up to. Jesus, that's the absolute worst
—an Indian do-gooder. That's when I joined my people.
That's when I recognized the enemy and turned against
him, slow and hard.

When I turned against whites I saw all my people—all
us Indians—as problems. We were all nothing but problems, and I got bitter about it to the point where I even
used to introduce myself as a problem. Some places I'd
walk into, they'd say, "What's your name?" And I'd say,
"I'm an Indian problem, how do you do." I was giving it
back to them real heavy—being very dirty, I guess.

But what do you do? How do you survive as a problem
when the enemy holds all the cards? I knew we Indians
were as good as anyone and I wanted whites to see that.
But I didn't know anything yet about the price of accept-

ance into white society. I was looking at Indians and saying, "Jesus Christ! this is really bad. We're drinking all over, we've got no jobs; man, more of us have got to get into the work force. We should behave properly." Then I got thinking about education and I thought, It's no damn wonder, we don't have good teachers on reserves; that's what's wrong. So pretty soon I was right out there making demands: If we had better teachers, if we had better doctors, and so on. I just totally lost sight of who we are. I absolutely lost sight of Indians when I got into the Indian business—the business of making Indians acceptable to whites.

When I got out of the Indian business eventually, it was because I realized I was just a person and there were other people—some of them Indian, some black, some Chinese, all kinds. And there was no Indian problem; there was only the white problem. That's how I saw it, and still see it. The people are there, too, those who created the problem, but they don't know what they've done, and I don't hate any of them for that. I don't hate anybody any more. But I had a couple more years of hell to go through before I got out of all that.

The Indian business! The problem business! It was like being back into that whole business life that I had left behind me in the Sault. I'd learned that whites just can't seem to help taking over and running everything, and I was bitter about that. But I still hadn't found a way to work and survive independent of white institutions and white organizations.

Whites seemed to have only one way of doing everything. You call a meeting, elect officers, form committees. You create an organization. So I attended meetings steadily, afternoons, evenings, weekends. That's about all

I did. And the whole measurement of the value of that was a doing thing, a busyness thing. I listened and observed, but finally I began to talk. It seems to me now that the things I was saying were not really very significant. But what matters to whites seems to be speaking out, and what I noticed more than anything else was that people began to come around. I'd known all those people for a long time and had some kind of relationship with them, but they'd never taken any particular notice of me. But when I began to speak out, they began to come around and there was this whole feeling of, "Hey, you know, this guy can talk." And they began to sort of push me up that ladder—the ladder you climb to become an Indian leader.

Well, I got better and better at speaking out. Became a popular speaker, in demand. Got higher and higher up the ladder. I began to really believe I was getting somewhere, getting to be somebody. And that experience of climbing the ladder was pretty exciting in some ways. I began traveling around a lot, going to conferences: conferences on housing, on education, on health, on religion, on economics, all supposedly having something to do with Indian people. I met a lot of people, hundreds of them, and I met some Indians because there were usually some present. Frequently I'd be asked to give a speech, and that meant going through the whole agony of writing it and, when I got up to give it, remembering what was written on that paper.

I was a very confident young man. But I wasn't, really, because none of that was me. I got anyone who was willing to help me with those speeches, and they were all carefully put together and written out. So hardly any of that was mine, really me. The idea, I guess, was to sound impressive, to put on a good show, and that's pretty phony. So I had the politician's fear of reporters; I didn't like to be interviewed or quoted. I guess I knew I was a fake and was afraid of being exposed. But sometimes a reporter would insist on talking to me no matter how I tried to put him off. So I'd go through hell trying to answer all his questions, feeling all the time that I didn't really know anything. But sometimes even that was helpful, because next day I'd read the paper and be shocked at all the bullshit and I'd ask myself, "Goddammit, Wilf, what the hell are you doing? Talking about Indians this and Indians that, and you know there's no such thing as Indians. There's only people." So I dreaded those interviews with reporters. I suppose I was afraid they might catch me, you know, because I was really involved in something that was . . . it was a performance. It wasn't me, so it was dishonest.

But at least I learned something from those interviews: reporters shouldn't be called reporters. They don't report. Few of them have any respect for accuracy. They have to write a story, not a report, that's their job. So if you don't give them a story, they take what you say and make a story out of it. Before I learned this I would try, really try, to tell them how I felt as an Indian person. Whatever opinions I expressed were strictly my own—I really emphasized that. I didn't represent anyone. But almost always they took what I said, distorted it into a big generalization about Indians, and turned me into a spokesman for Indians.

I don't know how it finally happened—maybe those newspaper stories had something to do with it—but somehow I began to hear myself talking. All that bullshit coming out of my mouth started going in my ears, and that really threw me around. That was when I started getting honest. I closed my eyes and just started talking off the top of my head. Nothing prepared; just what I felt at the time and only out of my own experience. And that's when I began to come down off the ladder. I don't understand just why that was, but it seems that when I got into sharing my feelings and experiences instead of making speeches people began to hear me. Maybe that scared them. Anyway, that's when the same people who had pushed me up began to push me down and off the leadership ladder.

I guess at first I resisted their efforts to pull me down, but then I began to recognize, I think, that I was really beginning to get somewhere. Not in terms of becoming an Indian leader or of doing something for Indian people, but in terms of my own realizations and of how I felt about Wilf Pelletier. I guess for the first time since I was a little boy I was getting to be honest with myself, getting out of the bullshit circuit. So a really significant element of excitement began to come into my life, and it was related to what was happening to me rather than to what was happening out there to Indians in the political sense.

I was lonely for a while. And sometimes when people I considered friends turned away from me, I was hurt. But it was good, too—it felt good. I had dropped a big load. Didn't have to perform any more. I could just be myself, and I was beginning to really like me. I didn't know whether I could survive just being me, but I was on my way to finding out. I was getting free.

6·The Way Back

I GUESS what I've learned—and it's taken me a long, long time—is that if you live in white society the most difficult thing to do is simply be yourself. No matter what pressures are put on you, no matter what you're asked to do, to simply be yourself. And that's because in white society just being born is a putdown. In other words, infants are not acceptable citizens. They're loved, cared for, and accepted mainly because of the expectations of the adults in their lives, and the expectations of the adults are that this infant will become somebody. Worse than that, that they'll make something of him. In white society there is no way people can be accepted just for themselves. It's almost as if there was a law against being just yourself. So that infant, as he grows up, learns he's under pressure to become somebody. And so he begins inhabiting all kinds of identities—schoolboy, errand boy, paper boy, boy scout, Sunday school boy—while he's growing up. These are all identities which are pleasing to adults, identities which adults equate with progress, development, improvement, all terms which have to do with the becoming of that person. He's becoming somebody, becoming something. And he goes on inhabiting those identities and outgrowing them like a snake outgrows and sheds its skins. Some people go through a surprising number of vocational identities, and very often they move from one to the other, not so much because they don't like a job or even because of economic advantage, but because of a search for an improved status, a better identity, higher up the ladder. And every time that person accepts a categorical identity, what he's actually doing is accepting an unreal self in preference to his real self. That's the worst putdown there is. The only freedom, the only health and wholeness, is when you finally come through all that, come out the other end of that whole bullshit thing and shuck off all those categorical identities, refuse to accept any more of them. Then you are simply who you are. You may be an Indian, you may be a Black, it doesn't matter. None of those things matter. What matters is that you are an authentic person and that you've finally become willing to accept and inhabit that authenticity. And that authentic identity is not a vocation, it's not a category, it's not business or profession, it's not racial, it's not Indian, it's nothing. You're Mister Nobody, Mr. No-name. But you feel easy about that. You accept that. You feel good.

I remember going to a conference in North Bay and I had to go directly from there to another, a conference on culture in Ottawa. I don't recall anything about the first conference. It was just routine—on housing, I think. But driving up from North Bay to Ottawa, I stopped on the outskirts of some little town along the way just to stretch my legs and rest from driving. There was a sandbank across the road from where I parked and well back from the highway. It was really an old gravel pit, I guess. It was in June, and all along the top of that bluff or sandbank there were holes where the swallows were nesting. The bank was crumbled away so you could climb it, but it was thirty or forty feet high and got steeper and steeper as it went up. Well, there were some kids playing there, about a dozen of them. White kids, ten or twelve years of age. The game was to climb the sandbank. One kid would get way back and start running up the incline, then climbing and clawing his way up the steep part, finding handgrips and footholds, anything to keep going on. And of course, it would usually crumble and he would slide back. But if it didn't and it looked like he was going to make it all the way, the other kids standing down below and watching would make a rush, claw their way up to the climber, get hold of his leg, and pull him down. Then some of them would try, would continue on up. The whole game was really one of preventing anyone from getting to the top. Somehow, I was fascinated by this dusty contest. I watched it for a long time. Finally a tough, wiry little guy made it all the way, and I really admired him. My heart went out to him. I felt like applauding. There he stood, triumphant and all alone. Then he began strutting along the rim of the bank, yah-yahhhing, shouting curses at the failures below him. When anyone climbed high enough to get a grip on the grass at the top of the bluff, he would be waiting to kick at their hands and throw sand in their eyes. Then I hated him. I wanted to sneak around the back way and push him off. Well, watching that whole thing really shook me up. As I drove on to the conference I couldn't get it out of my head. There was some pretty heavy symbolism in all that for me. I recognized it, but I wasn't ready to accept it. Not yet. Then another disturbing thing happened to me in Ottawa.

A lot of Indian people take tape recorders to conferences, to record the proceedings. Or maybe they do it just because they happen to own a recorder. Anyway, some of us were sitting around one night in a guy's room drinking, talking, and having a good time, and someone started playing back a tape he had made that day. Suddenly, I heard myself speaking on the conference floor. Others spoke too, but I got up and spoke two or three times on that tape. I spoke with feeling and passion. I heard myself telling those people what was best for them. I heard myself saying I knew what was best for my people. I was amazed. There was a whole disembodiment to that experience so that I could scarcely associate myself with the voice on the tape. It all sounded so foreign, so insane, that I found myself sitting there, thinking, Can that actually be me, saying those things?

That was a stiff jolt. And I needed it to realize how far gone I was, how degenerate and insane. Who was I really trying to help, my people or myself? I thought of all those women do-gooders I had always had such contempt for, wanting to help us poor Indians, filling their personal psychological needs at the expense of the Indian people. Calling it something else. Hypocrites! No one knew better than I how destructive all that altruistic bullshit was. But was I any better? Why was I so desperately trying to claw my way to the top? Get on the executive, get more power, become somebody. Didn't I like and respect the somebody I was? And if I did, why all this struggle to become somebody better?

Well, that was the bait, I guess, and I had taken it and gotten sucked into that whole power-struggle mess. And that madness—I think it is madness—I could see that it was not just going on in me; it was part and parcel of all of Western society. What Western society is based on, really, kept going by the people we honor most. The politicians, for example, who never really do anything except bullshit the people. And the wealthy businessmen who really don't do anything—not in Canada, anyway—except exploit the environment. But they were successful, damn it. They had made it to the top, triumphed over everyone. But when it came to honoring them, there was that hypocrisy again. They were not honored as ruthlessly successful competitors, they were honored as great leaders who had made selfless contributions. They should have been dishonored, I could see that. Really exposed and put down for the things they actually did in their lives: the public property they laid waste, the lies they told, the friends they used and threw away. People who fight their way to the top are the loneliest people in the world. If they knew what they were doing, not one of them would do it.

There is enormous pressure on everyone in Western society, including Indians, to succeed in that sense. I could see all that and I could see what I had been trying to do. And what a sad discovery that was! Become top Indian—an Indian leader—an Indian spokesman. Jesus! I was insane. And those things were only stepping stones. Recognition by the white community, that's what I was really after. But the price—that's what I hadn't realized. The price was losing my own people. The acceptance of my own people must have seemed pretty cheap to me at that time because I'd been willing to risk that—and my very life depended on it—for recognition and acceptance in the white community.

It's funny, but in that process of losing sight of my people, I began to find them again. It was a painful comeback, and it was slow. I continued going to conferences because I was committed and also because there were

Indian people there. But I didn't make any speeches, didn't speak on the conference floor. A lot of people were concerned about that; some were even pissed off with me. But I didn't care—I let them think whatever they were going to think. I'd sit around. I'd see a man just sitting there doing something with his hands, maybe carving something. He'd be in the conference and he wouldn't say a word through the whole thing. And I'd see others just walking around, visiting. They'd go listen here, go listen there, then they'd break up into groups, big groups, and I'd sit in those groups. All Indian people. And I found they had come hoping to learn. There were none who knew anything, none who came there to teach or tell others. "I came here to learn something, to listen, not to talk"—that's what they'd say. And you couldn't get them to talk.

That's one thing I noticed, and it really made me feel foolish. Me with my big mouth blabbing off, deliberately joining every damn club and organization that had any connection with Indians, running off to conferences all over the place. Well, I kept on going to conferences, but I shut up. Once again I quit talking, but this time it was the big-time public speaker who dried up. Once again I decided to just listen. I thought I would try to learn something too. And I did learn something. First I found that the more I listened, the less I learned. There was a time when I believed most of what I heard. I took it for granted that experts—any expert—knew what they were talking about, and that if I didn't understand them it was because I was dumb. I had never heard of gobbledegook; I didn't know that nobody can understand bafflegab. But now I discovered that most of the people doing the talking didn't know anything—had no idea what they were talking about. I found that few people spoke from personal experience. It was like a formula: The greater the education, the less the experience. So that usually the highly educated expert was not able to say, "This is how I see it because I have had such and such an experience." Instead, what I heard him saying was, "This is how it is because that's what I was taught." And backing all that up, there was always the inference, "After all, I spent twenty years studying this and I'm a Ph.D.," or, "I majored in this or that." But they had never experienced it. That's what those guys always left out.

I think people who are educated by experience tend not only to be tolerant of different ways of doing things and different points of view but to be curious, interested and intrigued by differences. Educated whites are just the opposite: they are threatened by differences. Simplicity is the key to survival. And observation: by watching carefully, native people learn all sorts of simpler ways to do things from other people, often from children. And of course, they are always watching whites, observing them very closely. And they talk a lot, too, about how the whites do things. And most of what whites do—they just shake their heads, let it go on by. But every now and again they see something, something they can use. On log drives, maybe, or working in the bush camps, you'll hear them: *"Nishge eshteget"*—"See, this is what the white man does." So the guys will stand around, watching: *"Neh! Gets-naw neen agutchtone"* (Hey, that's pretty good, you know). So they try. And first thing you know, they've adopted it, they're using it. But they've changed it, too: they're using it *their* way.

Lots of stories have come out of the north, particularly since the U.S./Canadian radar line was put in, about native people, mostly Eskimos, taking apart a complicated machine like a bulldozer or maybe a truck engine and putting it together again, without first being taught how to do that. Now, I don't claim to understand that, but there's one thing I'm damn sure about: they learn from just watching, watching a guy running the machine, observing. And all the time they're learning. They incorporate everything they see into themselves, make it their own. And I'm not sure I can explain what I mean by that. You see, there's no word in English for that kind of observation. People who are conditioned to get their information from books, conditioned to learn by submitting to instruction, don't know how to *look* and *see*, don't know how to observe. That's part of the price they pay for formal education. But those illiterate native people . . . it's like they can get right inside a thing just by looking at it. There's a totalness to their learning. And often their very lives depend on that kind of observation. All of a sudden a thing like a snowmobile comes into their lives, or an outboard motor. And it is sudden, because they are really Stone Age people, and not technically sophisticated. And yet in another way it isn't sudden, because those people are the best mechanics in the world. They can make anything out of nothing—that's how they survive. So when a thing like a chain saw comes along, they don't have to be taught a safety program. By the time they're through observing that thing, learning all about it through observation, that's in there too. Just built in.

Another thing is that with those people, learning is cooperative rather than competitive. As is living. One guy will see things that another doesn't see, perhaps. So pretty soon the first guy is doing better, cutting more wood with his chain saw, say, or catching more fox. But those differences never last long because they share everything, and most of the sharing of learning just happens through each man's observation. So it's all total. Corporate. The entire process of doing includes survival, includes safety for everyone. Those people are not fragmented or alienated by vocation, by doing. Doing is never just a part of life. Doing includes the whole man, the total community. Nothing is left out.

Listening to those talkers who never said anything, I began to wonder about a lot of things. I began to really think about my people. Then a whole reversal began to happen in me. Lights began coming on all over the place. I began to see schools for what they are—role factories for turning people into vocations. I began to realize that Indians are a very learned people. How else could we have survived? Suddenly I knew that learning didn't necessarily have anything to do with academic education or literacy, that my people valued intuition and knew how to sense things out, whereas white society puts all that sort of thing down.

I began to see that the selection and gathering of food, the preparation and the cooking of it, the whole feeling about food, were pretty different. And food was closely connected with medicine—all those herbs and the uses of them. I found myself remembering all sorts of things, things I thought I'd forgotten, and remembering them with a whole new significance.

The smell of my grandparent's house. My mother's father died in that house. He was bedridden at the last, and I guess my grandmother was often cooking up herbs and different things on the stove for him that I would smell when I came in. Those smells came back to me now, very strong, very distinctive. And the house. It was a very small log cabin. When you walked in there was a feeling of warmth—remembering it made me want to cry. Not just temperature, it was always comfortable, but a kind of feeling that goes right through you. I've had that feeling in a few other houses too—not many. Just beautiful. You step through the door and it's like the whole house puts its arms around you. What is that?

Those memories! They flooded my whole life for days on end. During my grandmother's later years most of the children in that community were helped into the world by her. She was always packing her little satchel, going here, going there, when someone's time had come. Of course, there were other midwives, but everyone tried to get her if they could. And when people died, the relatives would come and get her and she would take care of all that too. She knew everyone and loved them—maybe that was why. Nowadays all that is done professionally by a mortician, but I think it was better the old way. I think the dead should be prepared for burial by someone who knew them and cared for them. I never have been able to understand how anything as personal as a funeral came to be professionalized.

I think my grandmother was equal to any emergency. One time one of her cows lost its cud, and she got some flour and water and mixed grass into it and wadded all that up into a big ball of dough. Then she got some of us boys to hold the cow while she shoved that big ball down the cow's throat. Because if a cow loses its cud it will die. Years later I wondered how a cow could lose its cud in the first place. But my grandmother was gone then, so I couldn't ask her.

When I say that these recollections had a whole new significance for me, I guess what I mean is that I was really seeing my people for the first time. Seeing their morals and attitudes and values as compared with those of whites; seeing that my people were different from whites —very different—but that those differences didn't automatically make them shiftless or lazy or no good, let alone drunken or criminal.

Take theft. I could see stealing was really a sort of illegitimate exchange. Or it happened because the white system of exchange excluded—excommunicated—all those who didn't have the means to play the exchange game. In the white system such people became objects of charity—a real putdown—or they took to stealing, maybe a little of both. And there were a lot of them—the poor, you know. To me, that seemed to be a hell of a lot of people to leave out. Well, we had a concept of stealing on the reserve because the church was there, had been there for a long time, and they taught that stealing was a very bad sin. But it was really difficult for the people in those days—it's changing now—to make much sense out of that idea of theft because everybody owned everything anyway. Now I have to explain that a little bit, because everybody also knew there were certain things that sort of "belonged" to certain people. In other words, a man would build a boat or buy a fishnet, and those things were his. But in another sense they weren't his; in the sense that if someone else needed them, then it would have been morally wrong for the "owner" to deny him the use of something that was needed for survival. There were lots of spontaneous little games that used to happen around that whole thing, but never, so far as I remember, any of the white practice of renting or making deals.

I remember taking a load of manure over to Stanley Odjig's place one day in the spring of the year. I was helping him spread the manure on his garden when Omblase came along. We greeted him and went on working. Omblase leaned on the fence for a while, watching us, then came through the gate, and taking a fork that was stuck in the ground at the far end of the plot, began digging the garden.

Now when Omblase first came along, Stanley had just said, *"Ani,"* to him. He didn't ask him, as most whites would do in that situation, "What can I do for you?" Nothing like that; just "Hello." But he knew, just as I did, that Omblase needed something. So neither of us was surprised when, after a while, Omblase said, "I thought you'd be out fishing," Stanley winked at me: "No, Omblase, I don't expect I'll get out fishing for a month yet. Too much to do around here."

Well, this was the beginning of a long verbal game that went on between Omblase and Stanley for the rest of that day. But when Omblase left, he took Stanley's net with him. That's what he'd come for. And all through the whole thing both those guys knew that; both knew Stanley had a nice new net hanging in the loft of his barn; both knew Omblase had been winter fishing and had lost his net in the spring breakup; both knew that, eventually, Stanley would ask Omblase why he wasn't out fishing and that Omblase would then say he didn't have a net. And that then, of course, Stanley would tell him to take the one in the barn.

And I knew all that. But I didn't know why Omblase didn't just come directly to the point and ask for the net, and I still don't know. Maybe it was just our way of doing things; maybe it was all an excuse for visiting. But it was pretty common: I'd seen Indian people playing that game all my life. Of course, circumstances have something to do with it too. If Stanley's net had been down on the dock instead of hanging up in his barn, Omblase would probably have just helped himself to it and put it back where he got it when he was through using it. It was common enough for people to help themselves to things and replace them later. And that business of replacing or paying back in some way was sort of . . . I suppose the nearest thing to it in white society would be the honor system. But your acceptability in the community depended on that: you didn't take things and not put them back, or not pay back somehow. But you didn't ask permission. No one ever asked permission, as a matter of fact; no one ever asked that I remember. No one ever borrowed anything, and maybe this is why the whole idea of stealing was so hard to fit into that community.

A woman would come, knock on the door; the lady of the house would invite her in, and she'd come in and sit down as women do. She wouldn't take off her hat and coat. Of course, most Indian people never do that; they leave on their hat and coat. And she might stay for half an hour or even an hour and have a cup of tea, and they would talk, and then she'd get up to leave . . . and at that point her hostess would say, *"Ge go nah?"* (Is there anything?)

Then the other woman might say, *"Kah."* (No.) Then the hostess: *"Pakweshigun?"* (Bread?)

"Kah."

"Nebesh awbo?" (Tea?)

"Nah how. Bungee gwehta." (Okay. Just a little.) And so her need would be filled. She'd take her tea and go on her way. Maybe that was really why she had come. In any case, the onus was on the hostess to make sure about that.

Now, what seemed significant about that ritual, to me,

was that the visitor didn't come to the door and ask for some tea; she just came in and sat down. And the lady of the house didn't ask if she needed anything until her visitor got up to go. But to allow the visitor to leave without asking that question would have been a real breach of good manners.

The other thing was that the visitor would pay it back, but she'd do it in her own way. That was her privilege. One thing was certain: she wouldn't come back the next day and say, "Here, I'm bringing you back the tea I borrowed." What usually happened was that at some later time the other lady would probably need a couple of eggs or some butter and would come over, and they'd go through the same ceremony again. So there was that whole sensitivity to other people's needs that was present in the community. It wasn't necessary to ask for anything, because when you came people were always sensitive to the possibility that you might be there because you needed something, and they would question you about that. So within that community the idea, the necessity to ever take anything, to ever steal anything, was never there. There was never any necessity, because no matter what you needed it was available to you. But in these exchanges, of course, no accounts were ever kept and the onus was always on the receiver to make sure that no one who called on them ever went away in need. And that wasn't a business thing at all. It had to do with relationships; the desire to accommodate people rather than take advantage of them. And the result of this, I think, was that when people paid back a favor or paid back for something they had received, they usually overpaid—made sure they were generous. But the concept of paying back was not from borrower to lender but to *the one in need*. And I guess that was a sort of practical equality, a working equality in that community, because as long as people related in that way no one could ever have any more than anyone else. There couldn't be any rich people and there couldn't be any poor people because whenever anybody needed anything the resources of that community were at his disposal. They belonged to him. The obligation of paying back was certainly on him, but then there were certain people who couldn't pay back—everyone knew that. You know, there were old people and there were sick people, and probably some people who might have been institutionalized in white society but who were bona fide members of the community. But no one ever did without, it didn't matter who they were or what capabilities they might or might not have.

Old Indian people sometimes jokingly refer to the practice of sharing as "Indian insurance." Spelled out, what that means is that if you are generous in your vigorous years when you are able to give, it will all come back to you when you become old and feeble. They have more faith in that expectation than they have in the old age pension.

White society "takes care" of the needy too, in a token sort of way. Most of those who have do not sustain those who have not willingly, out of awareness of another's need, but because they're forced to do so. No one pays his taxes eagerly, without complaint. Most of those who give to the Community Chest or the Red Cross or whatever are shamed into it. And "charity" budgets are always inadequate. Contradictions! Most whites regard their society as the most learned and knowledgeable in history, yet it is the most ignorant. No people ever ignored each other so completely. Whites are so busy ignoring each other, they hire professionals to take care of the "business" of man's humanity to man for them. Makes you wonder who the poor really are.

I'm not old enough to remember the Great Depression of the early thirties, but I'm told that one of the effects of those hard times was that people became *aware* of each other, thousands of them. People cared for each other, shared with each other. Those who had surpluses gave away what they didn't need, lots of them. That's what I hear. Yet ever since, business leaders and politicians and experts of various kinds say we "recovered" from the Depression. And we don't want it to happen again. Stealing isn't the only white concept Indians have difficulty with.

You know, that time when I went and applied for welfare I was so simple-minded I actually believed I'd be getting help, professional help. I believed the people I'd be meeting would be all for me—champions of the downtrodden, so to speak. I thought, since they were on my side, they'd be eager to go to bat for me. Stupid! The fact that I had to go and ask should have warned me off. They disliked me before they ever saw me, that's what I found out. They suspected me of trying to defraud them, and all they cared about was satisfying themselves that I "qualified" for help. They didn't care about me or my need. Hell, they didn't even see me. And in order to satisfy them, to prove that I wasn't really a liar and a cheat, I was forced to discredit myself totally, as a person, as a man, as a human being. Then I could have my twenty-two bucks ... and come back for another dose of the same next week! That's sharing, white style. It's called charity, Christian charity.

So what it comes down to is that being poor or physically handicapped or unemployed is a crime against white society. I say such people are criminals because the treatment they receive is punitive. Their worst punishment is that they're given money—a little—as a substitute for compassion. In that community I grew up in I can't remember anything of the white concept of "making the criminal pay," "debt to society," "getting even with the wrongdoer," and so forth. All those things were incomprehensible. Nobody had any of those ideas. I can remember a couple of times when a guy got sent up for three months, maybe for drinking on the reserve or bootlegging or something. When he got out and came home, there would be a big celebration, a Welcome Home party—no stigma attached to that. And he wasn't a hero, either. He was just the victim of a misfortune—a minor one. It could happen to anybody.

The whole Indian feeling about the police and the law was that it was . . . well, it was "out there" in the great swampland of Whiteville and like most things out there, it was crazy. There was no way to make any sense out of it. It was just a big hairy monster that could reach out and grab you if you didn't watch out, and when it did, you were put in jail and charged and sentenced and then put in another jail. But you never knew what happened. Well, you might have a vague idea before the whole courtroom trip, but after going through that you were permanently confused. Most whites can't understand that courtroom lingo, let alone Indians.

I find it hard to think of punishment as related to that community I grew up in—social punishment. I suppose if the whole community had at any time wanted to punish one of its members, the way they would have done that would have been to excommunicate him. And they wouldn't have had a big meeting to decide to do it; it would have just happened. In other words, they would have turned him out; they would have freed him from the community, to speak of it in an odd sort of way. The white concept of punishment, since they don't have any community, has to be the opposite. Their means of punishing the wrongdoer is to "turn him in," to imprison him. In one sense the result is the same, because he too is cut off from society, but there the similarity ends, because that's not his punishment. He's deprived of his freedom: that's the punishment. The freedom to make his own decisions and act on his own initiative. He's totally controlled, reminded every minute of every day that he's not responsible, cannot be trusted. Told when he can get up, when he can go to bed, when to wash, when to eat. He wears a special "criminal's" uniform. He's exercised like an animal.

The penal system breeds criminality just as the army breeds war, just as all white institutions breed irresponsible, antisocial behavior. And I don't mean anti-establishment; I mean anticommunity, antipeople. And by "irresponsible" I mean unable to respond. Lacking in compassion. Unaware of the needs, let alone the rights, of other people. All white institutions are on a control kick based on distrust of human beings and human behavior. How are people to "become" responsible when they're never allowed to experience what that feels like? When all the important decisions are made for them? When ninety percent of the chance of taking initiative is removed? When even morality is defined and enforced by government?

I'm told that there's been a change lately: that the authorities are beginning to recognize that those criminals they have penned up are human beings. But they're still locked up. I've also been told that not so very long ago it was common enough to hang a man for stealing a loaf of bread. I find that hard to believe. Surely, *someone* must have noticed he was hungry. Maybe fifty or a hundred years from now people will look back and remember when the lawbreakers were sent to prison and the real wrongdoers were allowed so much liberty they almost killed the earth and everything on it.

Maybe more than any other thing, sharing was the basis of that community where I grew up. Sharing is a very fragile kind of relationship because if you ask someone for something, no matter how much you may need it, the possibility of sharing is destroyed right there. From that point on he may give you what you've asked for, or loan it or sell it to you, or he may refuse you; but whatever he does, relating has been downgraded from a spontaneous level to that of a transaction. And all deals and transactions are degrading. What you've done is rob him of his freedom, the freedom to see your need and offer to fill it —or perhaps not offer to do so. You've also robbed him of the joy of giving, of offering you something on *his* initiative. Now all he can do is fill a request. I find this is too subtle for some people to appreciate; they just don't see the difference. Finally, you've put him on the spot. If he refuses you he will feel mean; if he gives you what you've asked for it will be because you've asked, not because of his desire to give. So he'll have very mixed feelings about that—most of them bad—because his insensitivity has put you in the embarrassing position of *having* to ask. He is bound to feel guilty and ashamed, unless your need is not a real need, but only a service you wish performed. Then you have reduced him to a mere convenience, and he will resent your very presence.

I found I had a very great sympathy for many of the white people I knew because they sincerely wanted to build a sharing society but didn't know how to do it. They wanted to share but they didn't want to get ripped off. Maybe for them the answer is that you can't do it, it just has to happen, because they've grown up in a commercial culture where all relating with other people, with environment, with events, is dominated by deals and transactions. Totally. You take as much as you are able and give only what you must. That's survival! And that's what they are conditioned by, no matter how much some of them try to deny it. In white society, survival has been reduced to money. Oh, I know there's a lot more to it than that; there's productivity and technology and invention and science. But for the average Joe on the street, money is survival. And a job is money—simple as that. Survival is not in the land, the trees, the grass, herbs, roots, berries, plants, and animals. Not in him either, not in his hands or head, his instincts and intuitions, not even in his community because he hasn't got one. It's been taken out of all those places and put in the drugstore, the supermarket, the bank. Money in your jeans! If you've got that you can walk in anywhere and order . . . demand whatever you want. Walk into a restaurant and say, "Feed me." And they'll do it, but all you'll get is food. Walk into a hotel and say, "Shelter me." But all you're going to get is a plush cell. You can even walk into a brothel and say, "Love me." But all you're going to get is a piece of ass.

Thinking about those young people who want to share —those young whites—I found myself remembering when I first came to the city and how stunned I was by the waitresses in restaurants and the clerks in stores. They took your "order" and got what you wanted, but you couldn't get any kind of human response from them. It scared me. Except for the odd one, if you spoke to them about anything except the "transaction" they just mumbled something. They were like zombies—dead. That really bothered me. I never have gotten used to it.

I don't know how you're going to recover from that kind of conditioning. Maybe it isn't even possible. But I do know that survival is not money. The fact that Western society is not surviving shows that the reduction is not successful. You can be starving and naked and homeless, but if you have human warmth you'll make it okay.

Theft is taking something that doesn't belong to you —that's the legal definition. But that is only petty theft. There's a lot more to it than that. Theft is also taking possession of something that belongs to everyone, like the land and everything that grows and lives on it and everything underneath it. Theft is taking more than you need *now.* Theft is taking more than you give back. The earth we all share is like a joint bank account and we're going broke because there are too many withdrawals and too few deposits. Survival depends on mutual trust and . . . compassion. Sharing.

These remembrances I'm talking about were not dead. They weren't recollections of dead things and dead people way back there. They were all very much in the present and all very much alive. They were realizations all about me. I was in every one of them. No way I could distinguish between myself and my people. All those experiences I'd been through, not realizing what was really happening, what it all meant. Remembering them now was not just a recollection; it was more like a vivid dream in which I relived everything and when I "woke up" a whole new dimension had been added, a dimension of understanding. All that time my people had been telling

[176]

me everywhere I went, answering all my questions, but I didn't have any ears. Now I could hear them. It was like that.

I remembered being in a house on the prairies in the summer. We've finished supper and are just sitting around feeling comfortable. The women are cleaning up. The sun is about to set. No one is talking. The smokers are smoking. Tobacco is passed around. Sitting there in the darkening silence I am aware that a kind of communication is going on. A communion. And it's religious, deeply religious. But no one there would think of calling it that. It's all feeling, only feeling. A shared feeling of peace and happiness. A very deep contentment. Suddenly, my eyes are full of tears. The mother of the household joins us. The two oldest daughters sit just outside the open door, on the steps of the porch. It is night now. Stars are beginning to show through the upper half of the window. A lamp sits on the table but no one lights it. I know where people are sitting only by the glow of their cigarettes. Outside, the crickets are singing, and from somewhere far away I can hear a chorus of frogs. Then one of the men begins to talk. His voice is so low that even after such a long silence no one is startled. It's so low I can't hear what he's saying. But it doesn't matter because he isn't speaking *to* any of us. He's speaking *for* us.

I catch the word *gitamogasawin*, which means "How poor." How poor we are. He's telling of giving a bag of potatoes to someone, the last bag he had. Now he's telling about someone else who has a large family, a whole lot of little kids, and how poor that man is but that doesn't stop him. He still gives. He's always giving something to others. The neighbors come first—everybody comes first. All the people are poor but they always give to each other.

Listening to him, I think he's really saying, "How rich we are! We have so little, but it is sufficient. Enough so we're still able to share what we have, to give to each other. We are thankful for that."

There is a long silence; then another of the men speaks. He's telling about the truck he bought. Maybe it's the one I saw out in the yard under the trees, sitting on flat tires with the hood up and the engine all rusty. He says he was trying to do his best and he thought the truck would help, but it only made him poorer. But he doesn't talk about the gas he had to buy or the repairs or any of that. He says the truck took him away from home, deprived him of his family and friends. He says he had to do these things to pay for the truck. He also says life became very fast. He didn't see anything any more except the dashboard and windshield of the truck.

Then someone starts beating a drum, very soft, hardly touching it. After a while he begins to sing. The song, which has no words, goes on for a long time. It's like following a winding path through the woods in the springtime, up over little hills, down into ravines, and then swinging around and coming back. Always coming back where it started from. When the song is finished I know every inch of that path. No way I can ever forget it. The drum changes hands and another man begins to sing. This song too has no words, but somehow it is all about people. I can sense their bodies and faces—people in sunlight and darkness, talking and laughing, waking and sleeping. Children and old folks, all kinds of people, working, dancing, singing, their faces lit by fires. People living together. When the song ends I am crying. Everyone in the room is crying, and it's a long time before the drum begins to speak again.

So it goes. The drum moves around the room in dark-ness. A night of silences and singing. A night of prayer. When morning comes I'm almost surprised to see the faces of my friends once again. The mother and her daughters light the stove and make tea. It's like a whole delicious meal.

━━━━━━━━

Listening to a speech on poverty, my mind wand-ers off and suddenly I am back in Geralton. There's no reserve there, just a lot of people squatting on land outside the town of Geralton. Indians and Métis. I suppose be-cause I was a stranger, people kept saying, "If you want anything, if you're looking for something, or even if you're hungry, anything, it doesn't matter—go and see Albert." And they'd say, *"Awpechego gitch twawsah"* (This man is not poor, he's very rich, he's got everything). So I go to see Albert.

He lives in a little old shack just like all the other shacks in the settlement. The door is opened by an old man who greets me in Ojibway and invites me in. When he smiles I see that he has no teeth. The single room is heavily lined with tarpaper and cardboard. There is a little airtight heater which also serves as a cookstove. It's warm and comfortable. A shelf, two boards wide, juts out from the corner. On it there is an iron skillet and a sauce-pan. I am given the only chair; it has no back. Albert squats on an empty apple box. Behind me, a rifle leans in the corner. That's all. There's nothing else. He's got noth-ing he can give to anybody. I can't even see where he sleeps. Yet this man is considered the richest man in that community! We talk, about nothing in particular. There are long, unembarrassed silences. After a while he makes

tea and gets some bannock out of a big tin box which sits
on the floor at the end of the pile of stovewood. I watch
him shuffling around in his worn moccasins, putting
wood in the stove, dipping water from a bucket I hadn't
noticed at first. When he slides the stovelid aside, the fire
lights up his seamed face. His gnarled hands move slowly,
gentle with the tin mug and jam jar. I am drawn to this
old man. When his back is to me, I can see just where his
suspenders go over the top, how sharply his bones show
even through the thick mackinaw shirt he's wearing. I feel
like putting my arms around him. The bannock is really
good, the tea black and strong. We smile at each other over
the tops of our "teacups."

When I leave, after two hours, I am buoyant, floating.
I feel like singing. And I know those people weren't putting me on. Old Albert *is* the richest man in town, maybe
the richest man in the whole country. I have been with
one of the few, a rare one. Just to be in his presence is a
benediction.

I wonder what poverty really is. I expect there were
times when some Indian tribes starved or came close to it,
but I doubt that they ever experienced poverty. The
whites say poverty is a problem that can be solved with
money. I wonder about that, because sometimes I think
the poorest people have the most money.

Finding my people. That was like being reborn. It
was like finding life. I wasn't into speaking much any
more, but when I did get up and speak I found myself
proclaiming the virtues of my people, not defending or
justifying them like I used to. And I wasn't angry; I was
excited and jubilant, so much so that I felt I really had to
watch myself. I didn't want to become a self-appointed PR

man for Indians—that wasn't necessary. But I didn't care about white audiences any more; I wanted Indians to hear me. "Hey, look," I was saying, "this is who we are. And it's great."

Actually I wasn't going to nearly so many conferences any more. I wasn't asked as frequently, and I often declined because I was into other things that seemed more real—to me, anyway. But I had learned some things about conferences: how to really get something out of them and how to contribute something. And that is quite a learning. So now when I did agree to attend a conference, I knew beforehand that I wouldn't be going to many meetings. When I got there, I'd just sort of wander around, and I'd usually find some people in a room somewhere and sometimes I might know some of them, sometimes I mighn't. That didn't matter. It was usually in the evening and they'd be sitting around talking, having a drink, laughing, telling stories. So I'd sit down and join in all that, and it was really great. And then the next morning I'd meet them. They're all going to the first meeting, hurrying to be on time, and they've got big heads and they're sleepy and grumpy—not in very good shape. But they're going to that meeting just the same. And me? I'm just going to bed. Dedication!

So I'd sleep. Maybe not all day, but for a few hours, and when I'd get up I'd find my friends had finished their business and were about ready for some more fun. And of course, I was ready. Now, that didn't mean I wasn't serious about anything. It just meant that for me the real values were in people, not in issues, not out there on that conference floor. As a matter of fact, I can't understand why those things are called meetings, because you never meet anyone in a meeting. You're confronted by issues.

All meetings are like that. The same tragic thing happens in churches, in classrooms, in lecture halls, union halls, legislatures—everywhere. Instead of being able to socialize and enjoy each other's company, there they sit, in rows, all facing one direction, looking at the backs of people's heads. And they must be quiet, and serious, and pay attention to what's going on up front. And the reality, the fact of those people being there *together*, is missed. Totally passed by. Instead of being free to *do it*, they have something *done to them*.

Wherever people are gathered together, that is worship. It doesn't matter whether that gathering is in a church or a playground or a bar or a dance hall; the important thing is that the people are aware of one another and enjoying one another's company. That is worship and that is the real church. And when people are assembled under any other circumstances, having something done to them, that is sacrilege.

I think the church is conning people. I think it's taken the need of people to be together and turned it into a weekly lecture on morality. I still enjoy going to a Catholic mass. The atmosphere, the music, the whole bit can be very beautiful. But I don't think ritual should be a performance and make you feel like a spectator. It should include you; you should feel like a participant. I find that Indian religious rituals and ceremonies, wherever I go, are inclusive. That's the most moving thing about them, the feeling, the knowing of oneness. Sitting in a circle, in a teepee, around a central fire, the social miracle you experience happens ceremonially.

But if you observe carefully, you'll notice that all social intercourse is ritualistic. People just make their own ritual, create their own ceremony as they go along. And the ones who are freest don't even know they're doing that. Simple things, like coming into someone's house and knowing by the way they welcome you that they're really glad you've come. And the lady of the house goes and gets some fresh bread that she just happens to be baking out of the oven, and cuts off a thick, crusty slice of that beautiful stuff and puts butter on it and gives you something she's made with her own hands. And there's just something about the way she does all that that tells you it's a real token of love. Then she goes and gets out some of her preserves that, again, she's prepared with her own hands, and she serves them up for you in one of her prettiest dishes. A remembrance of last summer to go with that nice hot bread. Now, I don't see how you could find any experience more religious than that one or any ceremony more meaningful.

I think making things for yourself and for others—that experience of holding survival in your own hands and in your own skills—is a very spiritual, a very religious thing. And people who live like that are truly religious. They're the only real materialists left. And there's a very old ceremony about all those things. There's a certain *way* to smoke a ham or cook clams or make jam or split shakes. All those things are old, very, very old. And people never worked at them alone. They did them together.

There was a time when, in order to visit with people in various parts of the country, I had to have an excuse. There had to be something "important" happening, like a conference or a big meeting, to sort of justify the unimportance of visiting and socializing. Now I don't pay any attention to that, not any more. If I feel the urge to visit with someone in Winnipeg or Vancouver or Thunder Bay or Montreal, I just go. Because I've found that just to see people, never mind conducting business, is far more important, more productive of great things happening, than any other activity. And this is honest behavior, whereas the way I used to do things was dishonest.

I learned something else from going to conferences: how to put bullshit to some good use. Bullshit is a stimulant. In the ground it's good for making things grow, and I found that sometimes it could make things grow in your head. I would go to a conference occasionally—and I still do—but I went to visit with people, not to attend meetings. But sometimes someone would say, "Oh, I think you should go to this one this afternoon. This guy's really good. He's an expert and should know what he's talking about." So I'd go and there I'd be, listening to some guy sounding off, and it would be just too much. The bullshit would be flying so thick and fast I'd feel myself getting mad. But instead of getting up and arguing with him like I used to, I'd just cop out. It was sort of like playing hooky. I'd just goof off in my head somewhere—trip out. I called it going fishing. And when I did that, I'd start getting all kinds of really great insights into that thing he was bullshitting about. Sometimes I'd get so excited I'd have to leave and go to my room so I could really get into that whole thing without being disturbed. Then I'd start remembering things, all kinds of little things I'd seen Indian people do or heard them say, things that confirmed what I was now seeing for the first time.

The first time that happened to me, I was at a conference on housing. A lot of people were sitting around talking about housing for Indians. Most of them were white, so once again they weren't asking the Indians what they wanted. They were deciding, without consultation, what was best for those poor natives; deploring the tarpaper shacks and the outhouses; saying the Indians need running water, the Indians need bathrooms, the Indians need electricity and . . . oh Jesus! Well, a lot of incredible things have been done in the name of housing. Whole populations have been moved from where they've lived for generations to "better" building sites, closer to the power line or on higher ground or with access to better water. Those tarpaper shacks have been bulldozed and burned so the people who kept moving back into them would *have* to live in the nice new ticky-tackies Indian Affairs had built for them. It never seemed to occur to anyone that those shacks were *homes.*

By and large, Indians have never taken to Western European–type housing, and when they're forced to adapt to it they do some annoying things. Indian Affairs will build a whole row of houses and then supply the paint for them. The idea is that each resident is supposed to paint his own house. Well, a year later, or two or three years later, that paint will be still sitting in a shed somewhere and those houses will be turning grey, weathering in the rain and sun. With few exceptions, you can always tell an Indian village: the houses aren't painted. Or they'll move into one of those new houses and tear out all the partitions. That's not vindictiveness, it's instinct. It just happens: a door here, a bit of wall there, and pretty soon all those little rooms have been transformed into one big room. I guess most Indian families are *families,* not collections of individuals. Maybe they experience the privacy of cells as isolation.

Anyhow, I'm sitting there, thinking all these thoughts about Indians and houses, and suddenly I'm way out on the prairie. It's spring. The crocuses have come and gone. The last of the snow has melted. The mud is drying and cracking in the sun, and the Indians are moving outdoors.

Some are still sleeping in their houses, but almost all of them have moved the stove outside. They've put it in amongst some poplars or saskatoon berry bushes to shield it from the wind, and they've got some kind of canopy rigged over it—an old piece of canvas—or some have cut branches with the new leaves on them and made a sort of thatch. Most have made a rough table out of boards. There's a canopy over that too. And I know they're having their first feeds of dandelion greens and lamb's-quarters and nettles. It's changing now, but it used to be that people were all starved for greens by the time spring came round. Every place I go I see mattresses lined up and leaning against the sides of houses or propped against fences, airing in the sun. Blankets hung on rope clotheslines are flapping in the wind. There are a few tents, but most places just have lean-tos. It's great. It's like the last day of school. The people are free, and only the first snow will drive them back indoors.

And fires. Everyplace I go there's a little campfire burning. Not for cooking—they have the stove for that. The fire is something else. The fire is comfort, Indian style. If it isn't cold enough to be needed physically, it still fills a psychological need. It's burning away there most of the time, day and night, just a little fire. People going by throw stuff on it. No one really tends it. Sometimes it goes out. In the evening, the family gathers around it, the children, the old folks and parents. Frequently there will be visitors. There is lots of laughter and talking. Someone may get out a drum and sing some songs. I think most Indian people relate to that fire more than any other thing. It's the touchstone of tribal life and they take it with them wherever they go. When I was a kid I always knew when there was a guy working in a field somewhere or when they were cutting pulp in the bush: you'd see the smoke going up. There's the guy all alone in a twenty-acre field, and way off in the corner of it he's got that little fire going. He throws something on it now and again, but he doesn't stand around and watch it. Sometimes he makes tea on it. And when he leaves he just spreads it out, like that—doesn't wet it down, just sort of spreads it out with his foot, and after a while it goes out. I never knew one of those fires to start up again or get out of control. But then, none of those people build fires in the wrong places.

Those guys who run traplines in the winter and are gone from home, sometimes for weeks, all alone, the fire keeps them alive, keeps them from dying of loneliness. You know, comfort is not something you can have alone, in solitude. That's why solitary confinement is such a terrible punishment. Comfort is a social thing, a space you share and enjoy with others. And so he sits there, that trapper, at night, with nothing but bush for miles and miles, and he's comfortable. And what I think happens is that the fire assembles his family and friends. The fire is so strong, so firmly established as the center of tribal society, that it draws the spirits of all those people like a magnet and they are there, right there around that fire every night.

And the whites have lost that fire. They had it once but they let it go. Replaced it with a thermostat stuck on the wall. Think of that! That's a heavy price for convenience. All urban people have lost it, the common, the central source of radiance and comfort. It's like the very heart of community has stopped beating. Maybe that's why community is dead.

Listening to those guys planning housing for Indians, I just knew that in the old days hardly any of those tribal

people ever really lived indoors, even in winter. They
kept their stuff in those teepees or whatever, and they
went in there to sleep or if they wanted to sit around and
do a ritual or maybe just talk. But their activities, their life
—all that happened outside in the open. And maybe it's
in this sense more than any other that whites seem to be
just the opposite to Indians. Whites seem to be threatened
by the out-of-doors, at war with the wilderness. I know
that's a big generalization and there are exceptions to it,
lots of them. But just the same, most whites, when they
step out of their automobiles, unless it's in the city or a
manicured park, behave like aliens. I've known farmers
who never became conscious partners of nature, guys who
farmed their whole lives and every day of it was a fight
against nature. They even seemed to cultivate the land as
if they hated it. And they were always cursing the
weather—the weather never suited them. I guess God
should move over and make room for those kind of guys.
Put them on the board of directors.

I don't see how those two racial characteristics can
ever be reconciled, but if you're going to *live* in the Americas you'd better get with it. Stop the war and begin cul-
tivating the partnership. Get it through your head that
nature really *is* the great sustaining mother. You can't be
a European alien and survive in the Americas; you've got
to become Americanized. That means recognition and
acceptance of the values, the life-view of native Americans
—the people who learned how to live *in* this land, not on
it like parasites, countless generations ago. I really believe
that. European immigrants have been trying to import
Europe into America ever since they first started coming
here. But it won't work. It's taken over four hundred
years—that's really not very long—but the evidence that

it won't work is now beginning to accumulate with a vengeance, really piling up. People, especially young people, are beginning to realize what we Indians have always known: the Great American Dream is a nightmare. The truth is that most of those immigrants and children of immigrants never have lived in America. They've lived, and still live, in a *house* in America. And they don't ever have to go outside if they don't want to. Everything is piped in: that's the essence of white housing. Hell, they don't even like to be outside when they're outside! When they travel they get in that hermetically sealed little house with wheels on it and glass all around and they travel in that. They're not outside. It's all heated, all air-conditioned, there's music in there. They've got to take everything with them. That refuge has got to go with them just like a turtle's shell.

7 · No
Foreign Land

I'VE BEEN talking a lot about what I call remembrances at that time in my life. But the word "remembrance" doesn't quite cover what I mean. It was like coming out of a fog where I couldn't see anything into bright sunlight where I could see very clearly. Out of falsehood into reality, that's what I mean. You see, there was a time when I used to go to church quite regularly, and I went to political meetings and lectures and things like that at that time too. I guess I was pretty serious—I wanted to learn. So when I went I paid attention. I listened. And I did learn a lot of things in the area of what you might call great ideas and great thoughts and so on . . . philosophy. But even that, I came to discover, even that is mostly bullshit. So I was lost before I was thirty years old, wandering around in a fog of half-truths and falsehoods. I knew that, but I didn't know what to do about it—where to go or how to get out of it. Then one day I came bang smack into reality. I suppose it sounds silly, but what happened was that I saw a dandelion. Here I was, a middle-aged man surrounded with dandelions all my life. Then I saw one. But there was nothing that stood between me and that dandelion, that's

[190]

what I mean: no classifications, no categories, no words, not even the word "dandelion." Nothing. And that dandelion was not just a thing, one of a million yellow things that were bright and pretty and very common. That dandelion was a being, a living being that accepted and included me totally. I felt like I was standing in the center of the sun with those cool yellow petals going out from my feet and away into the distance forever.

I said I saw a dandelion for the first time. But it really wasn't the first time. I learned that too because there was a flash of remembrance in that experience—no when or where, just a flash—but enough so I knew that when I was a very young child I lived in that reality all the time. Those remembrances of reality began to happen to me more and more often and they were all about just simple things, really very little simple things, and none of them ever lasted very long. But they were what I lived for.

I suppose lots of people have experiences which actualize their identity, their totality. Experiences of oneness with the earth. I remember hearing a man singing in the middle of the night. Everyone was asleep, and way off somewhere he was singing. Indian singing—chanting. He had no drum, just the voice. And the voice seemed to go down into the earth and shake the earth and come up into me. And that experience was an experience of oneness. I've had that experience, too, hearing a wolf howling, and like the Indian singing, the song of the wolf has no words. And the feeling it gives me also has no words.

I expect that's when I began to really see the difference between what I now call "the bullshit circuit" or "the movie," that whole abstract world people are manufacturing and manipulating all the time—between that and the happening or flowing world I call reality. And the way that came about . . . maybe I don't know the word . . . I'm not sure, because I think I always had those feelings but wasn't aware of them. But it was a whole feeling thing. I've changed, you see, and before that change happened to me I used to have to make decisions; had to weigh all the factors one against the other, the advantages and disadvantages, consider the issues—was there money involved, and jobs. All that. And I was hog-tied most of the time. I spent most of my time and energy in just *trying* to reach decisions, trying to decide what to do, arguing it all out, threshing, hammering it all out with other people, and with myself in my own head. Man, what a violent, noisy process! Now the only time I get on that trip is when I forget that I can *know*. My feelings will tell me. The flow of my feelings—what I call energy—will take me where I need to be and involve me in whatever is happening there. To be where it's at, to know instead of guess, I don't have to do anything except go with that flow. When I forget that, then I begin to experience tension, anxiety, the stress of resisting the flow. And that's how I know I'm back at it, trying to *do it* instead of just *being it*.

So more and more I'm learning to feel my way through each day instead of trying to calculate my way through it. And I'm learning that the things that happen are almost always far better than anything I might have planned. That doesn't mean I don't use my head; it just means my head is learning to serve my feelings instead of suppressing them. Maybe that's what faith is all about.

But it's not easy. Something will come up and I'll sit back and ask myself, "Now, how do you really feel about that?" And sometimes I have very mixed feelings because that thing that has come up involves other people and I'm all for those people or that person. People are where it's really at. But what they want to do, or are doing—that may be another matter. I guess what I'm really talking about here is organization. I think it's great for people to be free to do their thing and I'll do anything I can to help them do that, but then all of a sudden that thing they want to do becomes a project, all programmed out, budgeted; committees are formed, briefs are written, they're into funding, and they're no longer doing their thing, they're all running around serving and feeding a monster they themselves created. Somehow the project has become the primary thing and the people are subject to it. And then I feel like a damned hypocrite because I can't support that. My feelings for the people haven't changed; that project is going to go on, and God bless them, they can go ahead and do it. But that's no longer where I'm at.

So I guess I'm becoming less and less useful to all those people who are into doing big things, more of a hindrance than a help. I have a lot of ability and know-how, and I have good ideas, sometimes, and I like to contribute those, but more and more I find myself just being written off. Like, someone will ask me to attend a meeting—to be honest, I don't go to meetings any more unless I just can't avoid it—and I'll go and I'll be sitting there, listening very attentively, and as I listen I begin to get this feeling that the whole trend of the discussion is pointless, just a lot of nonsense. And I look around at the other people, almost expecting to see by their faces that they're aware of the same thing. Usually what has happened is that my attention has shifted from whatever is under discussion to the assumption that all that discussion rests on. Maybe everybody is talking about schools and education—all the aspects of education—and I'm sitting there feeling very strongly that all schooling is a putdown, that the whole

[193]

theory of teaching is a myth; that there is only learning.
Or maybe a project is being planned that is going to involve a lot of Indian people—a "good thing" for Indians.
And I'll begin to feel that what's really going to happen
is that a lot of Indians are going to get assimilated. So I
have a hard time, because there seems to be an unwritten
agreement that you must never question the assumptions.
Then when I get up and try to express my feelings, as I
sometimes do, I guess people see my behavior as a viola-
tion of that agreement, and what I have to say comes out
totally opposite to the trend of the discussion.

After I sit down, there is usually a period of silence.
Nobody speaks. Then somebody will say something like,
"Well, I think we should certainly take into consideration
what Mr. Pelletier has said." Then maybe someone else
will ask what time it is, and say, "I'm sorry, but I only
have half an hour before I have to be somewhere else."
The whole thing is, On with the meeting, let's get on with
the meeting, and there doesn't seem to be any interest in
considering the point I've brought up. I'm just written off,
right there. There's just no point in talking about what
I've had to say.

So I guess I'm out of it, getting out of that whole
game-playing scene. It isn't that I'm not good at it—God
knows I've had enough practice. I guess it's just that I no
longer have any enthusiasm for it. I've seen through it, so
I can't take it seriously any more, nor any of those roles
I'm expected to play.

You see, to be a good game player—a winner—you
have to be one-sided (lopsided), off balance, some kind of
a cripple. You have to be for some things and against
others; for some people and against others. The good guys
and the bad guys. That's why I call it a movie. All success-

ful competitors are driven by a sense of loss or lack—millionaires the same as paupers—which reduces self to the smallest, most exclusive, frightened and alienated proportions possible. I was in that lonely space for years, all wrapped up in myself—the smallest package in the world —so I know all about it. Then one day I wasn't there any more. The games were still going on and the movie was grinding away, but I wasn't in there any more. The space I had come into was outside all that frenzied activity. Not separate from it but surrounding it. Location requires a "me" at the center. The essence of the game world—the movie world—is that it is self-centered.

Perhaps that is a way of saying what had happened. "I" was there, but there was no longer an observer and an observed, no longer a "me" and "you," no "self" and "not-self," no separate and isolated individuals. There was only one inclusive totality which left nothing out. All those billions of polarized pieces of the movie somehow flowed together into one whole, and there was nothing left outside of that. It was all flowing. There was the *appearance* of stability, but nothing was static. And it was all living. Nothing was dead. Pure life-energy, flowing uphill as well as down, piling up in crests, running down in troughs—clouds and rain, mountains and valleys, passions and peace. And it was nameless. In that flow there were no categories, no classifications, no races, no words; only the crystal-clear feeling of knowing. And if I tried to conceptualize any of that feeling, tried to qualify it with words like "reality" or "totality," I left the flow, I was out of it, *bang*, just like I'd flipped a switch. But so long as I remained in that flow, there wasn't anything I didn't know. That was the feeling—I knew everything. And none of it in the past or future; it was all right there. But nothing I could put a tag on, not one thing. There were no words and there were no errors. A mistake was not possible. Everything was exactly right. Perfect. Beautiful.

After that happened to me I remembered Megwetabejic. That's what the people say, *"Megwetabejic"*—There's only one. There's only one person: Jemnitow, the Great Spirit. And that seems to be much the same in every tribe, in every Indian language. I had never really understood what they meant by that—it had always puzzled me. But now I knew it meant "That's who you are." There's only one, the inclusive individual, the self. I knew it meant that the spirit of that self—the Great Spirit—is great enough to blend all "selves" and all "things" in oneness. Great enough to recognize and accept its own totality.

So that's how I came, finally, to know who I was. Not only an uncategorized and unqualified Wilf Pelletier, but also inseparable from all others and all things. And knowing who I was, a lot of things began to look pretty funny. Like demonstrations, for example. I used to go on marches for Rights. I had externalized Rights; I had put them out there, in the movie, and let some "director" play around with them. Now I saw they belonged to me, and whatever I felt they were—the responsibility for those feelings—all that was mine. So I took them from where they were, out there, and brought them back here where they belonged. I had no problem after that. I couldn't march any more or ask government for anything or ask anybody, because they didn't have it; I had it. So there was no need for me to march any more.

And I took religion from where it had got misplaced, out there, and I brought it, too, back here where it belongs, where it functions as my heart functions every second of every day, not just on Sundays. So there was no need for me to go to church anymore. And I did the same with learning and with justice and health and marriage and all those feelings and functions of a man which *belong only to that man.* I took all those things back, and I felt a lot better, felt almost whole again.

Then I took a look around. I saw city halls, court-houses, houses of parliament, churches, schools, and universities by the hundreds and thousands. I saw systems—systems for managing the land, the air, and the water; systems for managing human behavior; systems for managing religion; systems for managing learning; systems for managing food, shelter, clothing; systems for managing love and procreation: a vast complex of carefully engineered systems. I saw millions of people working, not for themselves, but for someone else. I saw millions of people doing, not what they themselves want to do, but what someone else wants them to do. I saw the depressing evidence of a people who have externalized and institutionalized—in fact, have tried to standardize—the very nature of humanity. I saw a whole people who've lost the way of life and in its place have built a mechanical monster which does most of their hard work, carries their water, delivers their food, raises their kids, makes their decisions, says their prayers, transports them, "informs" them, entertains them, and controls the people it serves, absolutely. I also saw that the monster, unable to manage itself, was running wild, totally out of control, ripping the land to pieces, spreading poisons, filling the air with filth, dumping garbage and shit in the rivers and lakes and oceans. I saw all that, and I saw the people, millions of them, crowded together in cities, living side by side in towns, villages, rural areas. But I didn't see a single community.

Still, I knew of some. There were a few bona fide

communities left in America, all of them Indian or Es-
kimo. A community is invisible from the outside—just a
collection of people. But from the inside it is a living
organism that manages itself. Not engineered, not
planned; just growing there—a sort of happening that
flourishes or shrivels depending on the climate around it.
A community has no institutions, no agencies, no forms
of extraneous government, because *there are no departments
of activity.* There's only a way of life, and all the activities
are just naturally in that flow, all the things that people
find it necessary to do in order to survive. In the communities I was thinking of, the people know nothing of
Justice or Religion or Education or Equality or Culture or
any of those big institutional concepts. Their language
has no words of that sort in it. But the people themselves
are just and learned and religious and equal. Those people
don't even know they are a community. The word itself
has no meaning for them.

Another thing they have no awareness of and certainly
no word for, but which I have observed lots of times, is
something I have come to call community consciousness.
I'm not sure I can describe it except to say it's common
ground, a kind of corporate consciousness that is shared
by everybody in that community and used by everyone.
Maybe the best word for it is "trust"—a kind of trust that
people outside that community can hardly imagine and
which the people inside that community cannot name. I
think it must be closely related to the kind of consciousness you see in a flock of sandpipers. Fifty or sixty individual birds are all packed together into one dense flock and
they're going to beat hell, turning this way and that, div-
ing and climbing, cutting around in tight circles, and that
flock stays right together, stays the same shape all the

time. And not one bird runs into another. Each bird acts, flies, moves like every other bird. The flock behaves as one, one single organism. You can see the same thing in a school of fish and in some swarms of insects, too.

Now, I don't know how they do that, those creatures, except that *they* don't do it; *it* does it. And I think this same thing, this same sensitivity or alertness or whatever, is present in tribal communities. For one thing, work is shared and produce is shared. People survive together as a group, not as individuals. They aren't into competition. But they aren't into cooperation either—never heard of either of those words. What they do just happens, just flows along. And they're not into organization either; no need for it, because that community is *organic.* Wherever people feel the need to organize it's because the normal condition of their society is dis-organized (not together). But I don't think the Western European way of organizing brings things together anyway, in the sense of human relations. From what I've seen, it usually does just the opposite. It gets things done, but it alienates people.

Let's say the council hall in an Indian community needs a new roof—maybe that would be a good example. Well, everybody knows that. It's been leaking here and there for quite a while and it's getting worse. And people have been talking about it, saying, "I guess the old hall needs a new roof." So all of a sudden one morning here's a guy up on the roof, tearing off the old shingles, and down on the ground there's several bundles of new, hand-split shakes—probably not enough to do the whole job, but enough to make a good start. Then after a while another guy comes along and sees the first guy on the roof. So he comes over and he doesn't say, "What are you doing up here?" because that's obvious, but he may say, "How's she look? Pretty rotten, I guess." Something like that. Then he takes off, and pretty soon he's back with a hammer or shingle hatchet and maybe some shingle nails or a couple of rolls of tarpaper. By afternoon there's a whole crew working on that roof, a pile of materials building up down there on the ground, kids taking the old shingles away—taking them home for kindling—dogs barking, women bringing cold lemonade and sandwiches. The whole community is involved and there's a lot of fun and laughter. Maybe next day another guy arrives with more bundles of shakes. In two or three days that whole job is finished, and they all end up having a big party in the "new" council hall.

All that because one guy decided to put a new roof on the hall. Now who was that guy? Was he a single isolated individual? Or was he the whole community? How can you tell? No meeting was called, no committees formed, no funds raised. There were no arguments about whether the roof should be covered with aluminum or duroid or tin or shakes and which was the cheapest and which would last the longest and all that. There was no foreman and no one was hired and nobody questioned that guy's right to rip off the old roof. But there must have been some kind of "organization" going on in all that, because the job got done. It got done a lot quicker than if you hired professionals. And it wasn't work; it was fun.

In Indian communities, in the past at any rate, there has always been something that might be called the flow of public affairs. Everyone—grandfathers, grandmothers, parents, children, everyone—was in that flow. And leadership was implicitly in the direction of that flow; it was potentially in every member of that community. So there never was leadership in the Western European sense, any

more than a river is led to the sea or the air is led to blow
from the north or from the south or from any particular
direction. Actually, the management of public affairs was
unsegmented, that's certain. Unknown and unnamable.
It's true that the council did meet, but I suspect those
meetings were religious rituals rather than discussions of
public business. I suspect the council made whatever decisions were necessary without much discussion. They
probably sat and smoked in silence until each man *knew*
what to do. And that knowing was the same in each man.
But the little things, the "doings" by which the life of that
community went on, were never consciously decided
upon. They just happened through each person in the
community doing his own thing, managing his own
affairs without interference, and not interfering with others; making sure everyone else had the same freedom. It's
also true that sometimes certain individuals were selected
and asked to take what the Western world would regard
as a leadership position. It might be a wise man, for instance, if there was some urgency for the community to
have a vision or reach an important decision. Or a great
hunter if the community was hungry. Or an herbalist—
some woman in the community who knew all the herbs
if someone was sick. But usually there was no necessity to
ask these people to do their thing. The resources of all the
people in the community were available to everyone and
when there was a need, those who could fill the need came
forward without being asked.

Present-day council meetings are more after the pattern of white meetings. But there is still plenty of evidence of the old-time community consciousness in many
Indian communities when the chief and council sit down
together, even though the structure has changed and

they've been forced to adopt the forms of parliamentary procedure. They probably won't talk about the issues, the items on the agenda, although there is an agenda, all neatly typed out. They'll talk about the doings in the community. It's all the same thing anyway, and all those items get discussed in the process. And they'll talk in Indian. Then after a while the chief may ask for a vote on this or that item on the agenda. And some things will be passed unanimously, with no discussion. At the same time, the chief may have become aware that there is not full agreement on one of the other items. Maybe there is only one guy who is still differing from the others, or maybe two. But the chief doesn't ask for a vote and override that minority. Oh no, they're not that democratic. So someone will say: *"Pkawn do showam don"* (You see it different than I, and I see it different than you).

So the chief will say, *"Nahow aneshgege anendomun"* (Okay, talk about it).

So the guy goes ahead and explains how he sees it. And that's always from his own experience, never theory. And everyone will say, *"Geget"* (Oh yeah, yeah . . . so now we have two ways of looking at it). And of course that is better; richer than only one point of view. Then someone else will talk about the way he sees it: *"Mesuswe"* (Well, that's three). And then someone else: "That's four." But they still have to reach a decision, so they'll say, "Okay, let's try this one first."

So they'll take that guy's suggestion and sort of fit it to the situation under discussion, and maybe that looks pretty good. But they're still not sure because they can always see each man's way as legitimate: "So let's try this one." And they try that one too. All of them. And it doesn't matter how much time it takes—there's no hurry.

But that's what they do: they eliminate all the points of view, with everyone agreeing, till they come up with one. And that one usually combines all the best parts of all the suggestions. And it's unanimous. That's a group thing too, just like those sandpipers. Accommodation is instinctive. No one gets crowded out. There are no collisions. The whole group moves as one, and differences are valued and used to help the community get where it wants to go. That's a survival pattern. Without consensus, the *community* is dead.

In my experience of Indian decision making, the important thing is to *hear* the other guy—have respect for the way he sees it. The white process of reaching decisions seems to be just the opposite: with them the important thing is to put down the "opposition"—get *your* way accepted no matter what. I've put in many a weary hour in white meetings listening to arguments for and against, listening to a bunch of con men and salesmen all trying to sell their point. No matter where you go in white society—courtrooms, legislative assemblies, parliament, any kind of meeting—what you see and hear is a fight, a word war. "Agreement" is reached through disagreement. But it really isn't agreement, it's the triumph of the majority. So it seems to me that white people can never get things together. They are always split into factions, hundreds of them. Their democratic decision-making process keeps them that way. Every time agreement is reached a large segment of the population—the minority —is put down. Defeated. So there's never any real agreement. But there is a hell of a lot of bitterness and hatred.

In white society politics is a game that is played by elected representatives, and the electorate are more or less spectators who watch the contest and cheer for this side or that. But they're not participants. Politics is the administration or management of public affairs, and in white society politicians are people who get things done for the people, do things for the people. But I think more frequently they do things to the people. In any case, the people are acted upon.

When I first moved into white society I became very much aware of the use of pronouns. I had been speaking English all my life but never realized how these pronouns —*I, he, she, it, we, they*—separated everybody and everything so completely and even inferred a basic disagreement. Or so it seemed to me. In my own language there is no distinction made between "he" and "she." "We" is used instead of "I." So when I say "we," as an Indian in my own community, I'm talking about me. I'm talking about me in the sense of that school of fish or that flock of sandpipers, even though the context of that particular time or instance may not actually include every last person in the community. Also I'm talking out of my experience of life as a flow, an uninterrupted river of happenings, rather than out of my experience of life as a series of isolated events. All that is just there, implicitly in the language. If I want to talk about events, I'll find myself just automatically using English, or if I want to talk about organization or technology or business. English is a better language for taking things apart. Ojibway is best for putting things together. Maybe that's it. If I get to feeling hostile and I want to argue about something— have a word fight—I'll revert to English. Just do it. Never think about it. And you'll hear that switch happening all over the place if you listen for it. You'll hear it in pubs or bars, usually, when people have been drinking.

I find it very difficult to explain, but what I think those

[204]

little differences in language mean is that the people using them relate in a different way. I think I have a fairly good command of the English language, but I still can't make it say what I mean, particularly when I'm trying to say something about Indian behavior or the Indian view of life. I get to the point where I just can't go any further in English and all I can say is, "It's in the language." And that's not so much because the actual words are different, but because I can't use English without getting into explaining. It *makes* me explain—puts me on a whole explanation trip. When I use Ojibway, I just talk. The meaning is just there—in the words, yes, but also in the silences, the spaces between the words—and there is a whole sense in which the listener is free to take what he pleases from those words, create his own "explanation." The words themselves don't persuade any more than music persuades.

So I've learned a lot about myself and my people and about whites too, just from knowing and using two languages. A language, any language, grows out of the experience of the people who use it. So English (I suppose, like all Western European languages) is a language of organization, of instruction, of explanation, of classification, of analysis, of calculation, and above all, of argument. It is designed to deal with fragments—details and events. But it's a two-way street: language is shaped by the people who use it. That's obvious. But people are shaped by the language they use. That isn't so obvious.

I began to learn that at a very early age when I went to school and found that education was all about bits and pieces and fitting those together, "organizing" them in various patterns. And that was, quite literally, a shattering experience. Not just the school thing, but what followed. School was just my introduction to the white way of life, the organizational way, "bringing order out of chaos." When I left school I found that all institutions were into the same thing. Business activity was the same thing. Everywhere I went I found people busily collecting pieces and putting them together. They employed lawyers to help them do this and borrowed money from the bank in order to buy certain parts and so on. And I got into that whole thing myself, so far into it that I lost sight of the world of my childhood, which was neither chaotic nor disorderly and which just flowed as a single, unbroken unity. Completely lost sight of it.

What that really means is that I lost sight of myself. Forgot who I was. And that all happened through the power of suggestion. Hypnotism. The suggestion that you are a particle, a tiny human particle, apart from other things and other people, at odds with them. That seems to be just implicit in the English language and it's there all the time. Never lets up. Well, I came to believe all that. My world became a giant jigsaw puzzle and the whole desperate object of my life all came down to just one question: Where do I fit in?

The essence of the Western European way of life is achievement, the realization of goals and objectives. And a highly sophisticated system has been designed for doing that. It is significant that this is called an educative rather than a learning system. It is productive of specialists, experts in hairline disciplines. Its effect is narrowing rather than broadening. It suppresses consciousness. Specialists suffer from restricted vision. Their "discipline" forces them to see the world through a porthole, but they are under the delusion that what they see is all of it. So it isn't surprising that they feel deficient, less than whole, unhealthy. Nor is it surprising that they tend to feel their world is falling apart. Those people are scared stiff. They're driven to achieve, driven to hold their disintegrating world together, driven to *make* it come together.

Well, things are achieved in Indian communities too, things like happiness and peace and contentment and laughter. And they work too, those people, and get money for it and make everything they need. But it's all done through the *expression* of consciousness, a communal awareness of self and environment as one, of self and others as one.

In the old time, Indian children weren't split off from the community at age six. Their world wasn't systematically busted up into millions of little pieces. They weren't forced to reconstruct themselves into parts and components so as to fit into a jigsaw world. Almost all Indian kids nowadays are exposed to white conditioning—the official assimilation program. They have no choice about that because they're forcibly injected into it at age six. But I believe in the instinct of my people. From what I've seen, it's still very much alive and increasingly active. For nearly five hundred years my people have withstood the efforts of whites to organize them, whole tribes have been wiped out resisting that, so I don't think they're likely to capitulate now. They'll go through it, but I think most of those kids will end up rejecting the establishment, just like I've done. Just like almost all Indians have always done. I don't know where that will get them and I don't know where it will get me. But I have an option now that I didn't use to be aware of. And everybody has that option, though some don't realize it yet.

Two worlds: one I try to cope with and the other I like to inhabit. I don't know how I'm going to survive because

I'm not really dependable any more by white standards. But I'm getting freer and freer. I'm going back to where I was as a kid; what was called an Indian: unreliable, not-to-be-depended-on, irresponsible, no good, a bum. I've got long hair now, so I guess that means I'm a hippie as well as an Indian. And I don't know what else it means —like, you know, I must be dirty and I probably stink. That's what's happening to me and that's where I'm going. You can't be in that flow and in the movie too, not simultaneously. And all those feelings I find in that flow, and only there, are beautiful. I want that feeling of irresponsibility. That's the greatest feeling there is.

But whatever happens to me I'll have lots of company, Indians *and* whites, because the kids are dropping out by the thousands, out of the games, out of the organizational movie, and it isn't taking them as long as it took me. They've got a lot to learn, but they aren't wasting time any longer going to school, getting educated. They're learning. They're going back to the land, more and more of them. And that's the only real seat of learning there has ever been. They'll learn from the land, all they need to know, all there is to know. If they stay there long enough, they'll learn that they *are* the land.

I expect that may sound like a very strange statement, especially to anyone born and bred in the city, who's been walking on cement and asphalt so long he's forgotten there is any land. But those early explorers, you know, who accidentally "discovered" this island, what were they looking for? Land? And those immigrants who followed, millions of them, what were they looking for? Land? And how did they feel about America? How many of them said, "Oh, I'm not here permanently. I'm just staying for a while, long enough to make a stake, then I'm going back.

Back to the old country. Back *home.*" Those astronauts walking around on the moon, I'll bet when they splash down on their return to earth they're crying, not from relief, but from the joy of being back home. What is that? What's the meaning of that "home" thing? Isn't that who you are? Isn't that what it means? All those thousands of Indian people who go back to the reserve every chance they get, even for a weekend, even for a day, you know what they say? "This is where I like to be." That's what they say, but what they feel is, "This is who I am."

It takes a long time not to feel like an alien, a long time to feel at home, a long time to search out and discover who you are. But if you go all the way with that exploration it takes you beyond race, beyond color, beyond class, beyond every kind of category, and you find that you belong to humanity. And *that's* who you are. If you go all the way with that search, it takes you beyond property, beyond lumber, fish, furs, metals, oil, beyond "resource" industry, beyond commercial food production to where you find you belong to the land. And *that's* who you are. And when you are *that,* there is no foreign land. Wherever you are is home. And the earth is paradise and wherever you set your feet is holy land.

When you no longer go around accounting for yourself, making yourself understood, justifying your existence, when you no longer *feel* like an alien anywhere, you've come home. You know who you are. You've found your family, the human family. And there is no such thing as the human family and "others." Not any more. As long as you leave anyone out, *you* are the alien and that search for wholeness, for oneness, for who you are, has to continue.

And I guess that must be why young Indian people

leave the reserve and go "out there." That's why they keep
doing that. Everywhere except on the reserve they feel
like aliens and they don't like that, don't like being forced
to live on a social island. They want to feel at home in the
whole country, the whole world. What they don't realize,
what they have to learn, is that except in the very least
sense of the word, hardly anyone feels at home out there
—not yet. Minorities, classes, political parties, religious
denominations, races—all groups and factions are aliens
one from another. White society is a conglomeration of
aliens.

The young white people know that. That's why
they're doing just the opposite: leaving the urban scene
and going back to the country. Back to the land. People
won't accept them but the land will. They've found that
out. But will they accept people—all people—even those
who reject them? And will they accept the land? If they
will (and we still have to find that out) then there is hope.
Together, we may yet rediscover America.

I believe that anyone now living in America or anyone
who wishes to come to America can belong here. When
I say "belong here," I mean that it isn't necessary to buy
land and "own" property in order to belong someplace.
How can you buy something you've already been given?
Besides, the land is living; how can you butcher it up and
offer the cuts for sale without killing it? And the land is
sacred. You don't live off it, like a parasite. You live in it,
and it in you, or you don't survive. And that is the only
worship of God there is. When you buy land you are
dispossessed by the act of purchase. The whole transaction is a lie that says, "This is my land. It belongs to
me," when the truth is that you belong to it.

Those who belong here know this. They've always

known it. And they're increasing in numbers. The people who *belong* in America are coming home.

The earth is designed for animals. It's the home of animals. People are beginning to remember this, beginning to behave once again like honest and respectable animals. Every animal has its own unique pattern of survival—the spider its web, the beaver its dam, the turtle its shell. And man has community. The key to survival is in that flock of sandpipers.

I believe the people will find their way out of the maze of every disintegrating institution, every last one, out into the open once more. They're already finding their way out of the cities. They're rediscovering the land. The cities as we now know them will remain as empty monuments to death. But the people who honor life will live.

In the country the fences will rot and fall down by and by, and no one will rebuild them. And the people will stand apart, as trees stand free, that they may be together.

About the Authors

Wilfred Pelletier is codirector of the Nishnawbe Institute, an Indian educational and cultural project. He has long been involved with a group of Indian wise men who are concerned with ecology and the restoration of traditional Indian beliefs and customs. Ted Poole is a long-time friend and confidant of Wilfred's and is a consultant to the Nishnawbe Institute.